know YOURSELF

||||||||||||||||||

D1614953

know YOURSELF

Achieve Your **GOALS**
through better **SELF-KNOWLEDGE**

Dr Ellen Balke

KOGAN
PAGE

YOURS TO HAVE AND TO HOLD
BUT NOT TO COPY

First published in 1999

Kogan Page Limited
120 Pentonville Road
London N1 9JN

© Ellen Balke, 1999

British Library Cataloguing in Publication Data

A CIP record for this book is available from the British Library.

ISBN 0 7494 2900 3

Typeset by Jean Cussons Typesetting, Diss, Norfolk
Printed and bound by Clays Ltd, St Ives plc

Contents

This book would not have been possible without the support and patience of my family and friends.

Thank you.

1 The Start of the Journey

INTRODUCTION

Personal or self-development has in recent years become something of a fashion. There are many different forms of self-development but they should all have a few elements in common. All self-development needs to be achieved within a clear framework, giving the individual full responsibility for their lives. The process should have the ultimate goal of releasing the full potential of the individual. Working at personal development is much the same as sports training, the moment you stop training is the moment the benefits start to wane.

> Self-development and improvement is not a one off or quick fix solution, it is a way of life.

To continue the sports analogy, the best athletes are the ones who have worked through the difficult issues and have come out the other side of the pain barrier. They are the ones who know what fear is, can face up to it and deal with it. They have pushed themselves beyond what they felt was possible, and kept trying even when the odds appeared to be stacked against them.

Athletes cannot watch themselves in action and give objective assessments of what they are doing, what's good about it and what needs to be improved. They rely on their instinct and experience. To support them, most top athletes

1

have a coach who, through observation and suggestion, spurs them to improve.

Through self-development you can reassess who you are and who you want to be. You can regain the confidence that you once had as a child. As a very young child you probably did not spend too much time worrying about what others thought of you. You just were, you experienced events as they happened and took them at face value.

Self-confidence only becomes an issue when you realize that others have opinions about you, when you realize that the image you present is important. As you enter society you naturally want to integrate and to do what you need to play by the rules of that society. This is where right and wrong start to creep in. There are right ways to be and wrong ways to behave. There is the ideal you strive for. You start to compare yourself to what you hold as the ideal and usually find yourself falling far short of it.

Over the years your confidence gets eroded and you start to spend huge amounts of energy trying to regain the self-confidence you once had or, at least, find ways of generating the image that makes everyone else believe you have it. Gaining or, perhaps more accurately, regaining our self-confidence is about keeping things simple. It is about keeping others' opinions and thoughts about you in perspective.

Self-confidence suggests that you are able to trust in, and rely upon yourself. It doesn't suggest that you have to be perfect. So regaining self-confidence is not about getting everything right, it is about trusting yourself to be able to deal with life as it comes at you. Sometimes when you have a really close friend, someone in whom you have confidence, you might say 'I would trust them with my life', well, self-confidence is exactly that. Trust yourself with your own life.

There is nothing mystical or magical about the process of self-development. It's not a deep psychological analysis but neither is it something to be taken lightly. This book will introduce you to a clear and simple process of self-development that anyone can use to improve aspects of their lives that are not working as well as they could be. This book aims to be your coach.

Have you ever met people who do nothing but complain about problems, the people and the difficulties in their life? Or perhaps you know someone who consistently makes the same mistakes and cannot understand why they keep ending up with the same consequences.

Actually, this probably describes all of us at some point in our lives. When life becomes a kind of merry-go-round, you end up going round and round experiencing the same scenes each time you go round. Through self-development you can get off the merry-go-round and have a go at one of the other rides at the fairground of life.

If you want to improve the quality of your life then this book is for you. If you want to complain about life and its hardships then stop right here. If you are prepared to look honestly at yourself and have the courage to change what needs to be changed then read on. If not, why not give this book to someone else? If that sounds harsh it's probably because to get the most out of any self-development programme means you have to work hard at it. As in most situations, what you get out of it depends on what you put into it.

Well done! By choosing to read on you have just made your first step towards changing your life.

Probably the best way to read this book is to take a chapter at a time, do the exercises in that chapter and then put the book down for a couple of days before going on to the next chapter. You might find some of the exercises difficult to do at first and you may need to go back over some of them. You can work through the book alone or in partnership with someone. Remember, self-development is a continual process and you may need to go back and repeat exercises at times.

So where do you start your journey of self-development? Well, by seeing where you are now and how you got there. You cannot navigate from one point to another unless you know where both the start and the destination are in relation to each other.

YOUR PERSONAL PORTFOLIO

Creating a life map

A life map is simply a way of pulling together your personal history. Please take a few moments to think about major events in your life and then plot those events on your life map. You can do it any way that suits you and you can add anything you feel is relevant. Things that you might like to add are key events, how you felt about them, and how they influenced you. Figures 1.1, 1.2 and 1.3 are several different ways you can draw a life map. Choose one that you feel comfortable with or create your own style.

You can draw going up the page or along the page.

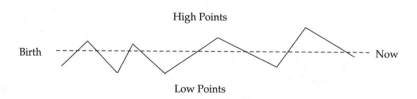

Figure 1.1 *A life map*

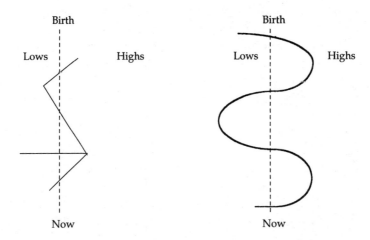

Figure 1.2 *A life map*   **Figure 1.3** *A life map*

Sometimes as you are drawing your life map you may feel things were generally good but a negative event occurs. As shown in Figure 1.2, you can show this by drawing a line going in a different direction from the general trend.

Figure 1.4 maps out your life using age as the determiner.

All the events you have just written down on your life map have had an influence on who you are and how you see the world. Equally, your future will be determined by what you do now.

If you want to change the future you need to work at the present.

Having completed your life map, ask yourself the following questions, how many lows are followed by highs? Who got you out of those lows? Was it yourself, or perhaps you had help from people who care about you?

Sometimes when you are at a low point you feel like there is no end to it, at this moment look back to your life map and remind yourself how you got out of previous low points. Also it is important to remember that all low points

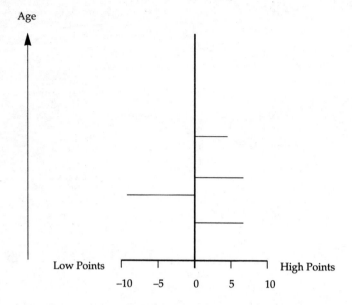

Figure 1.4   *A life map using age as the determiner*

You can draw your own life map here.

Figure 1.5 is an example of a life map.

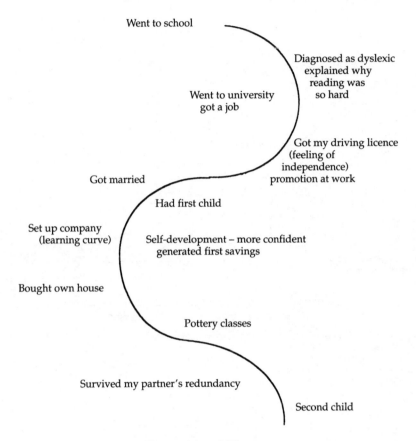

Figure 1.5 *A life map*

do come to an end and are often followed closely by a high point. In most cases a life map shows a lot about yourself, each event in your life is one piece of the puzzle and all the pieces make a full and varied tapestry.

Building a personal portfolio

Your life map has provided information about your past and how you came to be who you are. You need to bring that firmly into the present so that you have a strong

You can draw your own life map here.

foundation upon which to build your future. To keep this foundation in clear focus you need to build a personal portfolio. The word portfolio simply means to refer to a collection of items, something you can hold on to as a reminder of all that you are, know, and can do.

Now look back to your life map and think about the events on it. What skills did you use to manage those events? What have you learnt? Consider all that you are in terms of the qualities, skills and achievements you have developed over the years.

To help your thinking you may like to consider the following as definitions. Qualities are natural gifts you have, and you may have developed them more over the years but they come fairly naturally to you. Skills are something you have had to learn. Achievements are events that you have planned for, worked towards and succeeded at.

Here is an example of a personal portfolio.

	Professional/Work-Related	Personal
Qualities	Ambitious Determined Tenacious Confident Honest Integrity Loyal Team player Results oriented	Loyal Honest Tolerant Caring Faithful Supportive Energetic Adventurous Sociable
Skills	Understanding people Project management Negotiation Influencing Team building Meeting deadlines Communication Selling Presentations Strategic thinking	Golfing Tennis Cooking Tact Swimming Listening Creating ambience Planning Time management Stress management
Achievements	Setting up a business Learning about finance Degree Recruiting good staff Developing staff Selling large contracts Bringing five top clients to the business	Learning to drive Long-term relationships Learning about equities My friends and acquaintances Relationships with family Garden Charity work House

Based on your thoughts so far then, what do you have to bring to the party in your work-related and/or personal life? Your personal life refers to all the qualities, skills and achievements you have, or use, outside of the work environment. What has your past given you as a foundation for your present and your future? You may find that there is a lot of similarity between the work and personal sides of the table, that is fine because they will naturally influence each other.

Perhaps you have never worked or have been working in the home. Don't worry, this doesn't mean that you have nothing to put into the professional or work-related box. Let's say you have been looking after the house and children for some time. Think about the qualities and skills you use everyday. For example, you may need to use good planning skills to get everyone ready and out of the door in the morning, to collect the dry-cleaning, do the shopping and prepare an evening meal, while at the same time dealing with the plumber, the telephone bill, and so on. As you can see, there are various skills involved like planning, budgeting, negotiating, delegating and many more. Have you ever organized a house move? Think about all the skills you needed to do that.

Take your time to write at least ten items in each box.

Now fill in your personal portfolio on page 11.

How hard was that?

Actually, many people find this exercise fairly difficult. How many times did you stop and say to yourself, 'is that really a quality, skill or achievement?' or 'would others see that as an achievement?' You probably rarely take the time or the indulgence to take stock of where you are.

Most of you forget or don't acknowledge your qualities, skills and achievements. When you succeed at something, how often do you deny it was difficult or a struggle? Something tells you that if you achieved it, it can't have been that hard, or indeed much of an achievement at all. Your modesty doesn't allow boasting and as a result you deny or forget your own successes.

	Professional/Work-Related	Personal
Qualities		
Skills		
Achievements		

Going back to your personal portfolio, you might like to take note of the qualities, skills and achievements that overlap your work-related and personal life. Many skills you use in your private lives you also use at work and vice versa. You might see these parts of your life as separate entities. They aren't. They are all part and parcel of you and your life. There really is no need to be a totally different person at work or home!

Just to ensure that you haven't missed anything out, or if you are having real difficulty thinking of enough things to put in your personal portfolio, look at the lists below and see what you have forgotten.

Example list of qualities

courage	empathy	calmness
energy	dynamism	happiness
adventurous spirit	patience	tolerance
sociable nature	compassion	openness
honesty	ambition	integrity

Example list of skills

analysing	communicating	decision-making
delegation	encouraging others	influencing
selling	negotiating	organizing
planning	initiating	innovating
staying calm	joke telling	making speeches
learning	DIY	typing
house keeping	managing money	dealing with
driving	supporting others	problem solving
time management	cooking	educating your
listening	managing projects	children
report writing	completing things	learning languages
motivation	requesting support	leading a team
facilitating skill	sewing	risk management
teaching	managing your environment	
dealing with conflict	foreseeing possible consequences	

Example list of achievements

walking	talking
reading	first day at school
relationships	passing examinations
graduation	driving test
your first lover	going to university
your first job	promotion
marriage	children
giving your first good speech	standing up for yourself
balancing needs of children, partner, job	learning to fly
facing your fears	admitting your humanity

If you are still having trouble with either your life map or your personal portfolio, why not ask two or three people close to you to help you? It is probably best if you give them warning of what you want from them and give them some time to think it through.

BALANCING THE POSITIVE AND THE NEGATIVE

Think back to last week, how many times did you sit down in the evening and tell yourself how great you were that day? Of the ten things that might happen to you in a day, let's say that eight were good and two were bad. Which events do you think or talk about in the evening?

Do you sit down with a friend, or your partner, and tell them about the eight positive events or the two negative events? And what do they tell you about? Or maybe you don't talk about it at all because you don't want to re-live the whole day again? Whatever you do, you must balance the negative with the positive.

It's true, isn't it? What do you remember most about your life? Isn't it always the mistakes, the upsets, the failures, the embarrassing moments, or the time you made that dreadful fool of yourself? It's as if your memory meticulously stores up all those bad moments, and then throws them at you every now and then just to remind you of how many times you got things wrong. Use your personal portfolio to remind yourself of all the positive things about you and your life when they seem hard to remember.

The point is that if you do not know your own worth, your skills and achievements and what you have to contribute, who will? Most of us look for approval and recognition from others. That's nice but it does mean we are sitting waiting for the day they remember, or feel like, giving us that recognition.

> You need to take responsibility for yourself and acknowledge yourself.

Confidence must come from within yourself, not from others. We will look more closely at confidence building later but for the moment it is imperative that you suspend your critical self and see the positive aspects of yourself and your life. Most of us have confidence levels that don't need the added burden of negative thinking. Stop undermining the positive for just a moment.

I am not suggesting that you bury your head in the sand and ignore the bad moments or events but rather that you learn to deal with them differently. The process is quite simple really, but it takes a bit of practice. We will look at the process of handling mistakes later on in the book.

Now looking at your lists of skills and achievements, imagine that someone else had given it to you and said these are my skills and achievements. What would you think about that person? Would you like to get to know that person better? Are they interesting, could you learn something from them, do they have anything to offer to you? In all honesty your answer is probably 'yes.' Well, that's you, you're looking at, so give yourself some credit!

SUMMARY

At this stage you should have your life map which shows your personal history and your personal portfolio which shows all your qualities, skills and achievements. In other words, you are well on your way to beginning to see who you are, your worth and what you can bring to any situation. You have the foundations of where you are, the starting point for your journey. Please put the book down and take a break before starting the next chapter.

2 Understanding Your Image

Knowing who you are and why, will help you to create your future. However, the things you have written down in your life map and personal portfolio provide only half the picture. The other half lives in the realm of perception and the image you generate. You have some great skills, but unless you see yourself as having those skills, and can make others see them as well, they will stay locked in their box, never to be acknowledged. Being who you are is one thing, being seen for who you are can be quite another.

The first step is to spend just a few moments thinking about how you perceive yourself: write in the adjectives or phrases you would use to describe yourself in your self-perception box on page 18. Throughout this chapter please try to balance the positive with the negative for every negative adjective or phrase try to generate two positive ones.

How do I perceive myself?		
hard-working	driven	tough
enjoy good food	ambitious	afraid of failure
value my friendships	able	friendly
determined	professional	

YOUR SELF-PERCEPTION BOX

Complete as much as you can.

How do I perceive myself?

Building the full picture

The next step is to consider how you believe others perceive you. To do this you can create a perception tree, an example of which is given on page 20. A perception tree has several boxes describing different groups of people likely to be part of your life, each with a set of adjectives and phrases which that group of people might use to describe you.

The perception tree allows you to summarize all the different aspects of yourself. Each of you is like a diamond with many different facets that you choose to show or to hide. You choose quite carefully which facets to show to whom, when and where. The thing to bear in mind is that all the different facets make up the diamond and if any one facet is missing, the full greatness of the diamond is not accentuated.

Example of a perception tree

So let's see how you believe the world perceives you. Choose your groups of people for your perception tree and just write down the adjectives and phrases they might use to describe you.

If you are really brave you might like to ask people within each of the groups for the adjectives and phrases they would use to describe you. Remember to let them know exactly what you need and give them time to think it through. It is fine if you don't want to ask others, the exercise will also work if you do it by yourself. An example of how I believe others perceive me is shown in Figure 2.1.

Think about how you behave with each group of people you have chosen for your perception tree. If you were to ask them, what patterns of behaviours or actions might they bring forward as evidence to substantiate the adjectives and phrases in each of the boxes? People will determine their beliefs of you based purely on what they have experienced with you or heard about you.

It is your behaviour that creates your image.

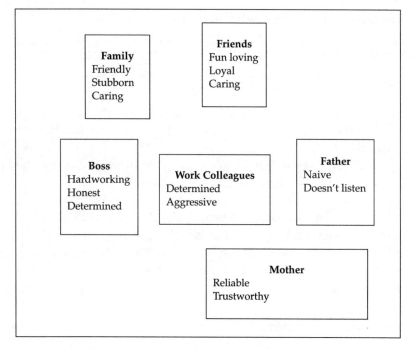

Figure 2.1 *How I believe others perceive me*

This is both the problem and solution to creating your image. On the problem side, people often make assumptions about your behaviour and consequently about you. Everyone does this, it is a natural process used to make sense of your environment. You cannot stop others or indeed yourself from making judgements.

As for the solution, since it is your pattern of behaviours or actions that generate assumptions and determine what others think of you, then, if you can change your pattern of behaviours or actions, you can also influence or change their assumptions and beliefs and therefore their perception of you.

I should say at this point that this probably isn't as easy as it sounds because you first need to determine the relevant pattern of behaviours, make a decision to change and then give the others time to readjust their views of you based on your new patterns of behaviour. Depending on

Now fill in your own perception tree.

Figure 2.2 *Your perception tree*

the length of the relationship and the depth of the feelings, this can sometimes feel like an uphill struggle. Remember also it is your choice as to what aspects of your behaviour you wish to address. As long as you understand why you generate the image you do, it is up to you what you do about it.

So if you are ready to have a hard look at what you do to generate your image then move on to the next exercise. Look back at your perception box and write down the adjectives you would use to describe yourself in the left-hand column and the behaviours or actions that earn you the image in the right-hand column.

How I perceive myself

Adjective	Description of behaviour
Honest	Admits mistakes, like the time the letter went out to Mr Jones
Determined	Stays with it until everyone else is ready to give in, the family outing

You may experience conflicting perceptions of yourself, this is quite normal as you may well feel and behave differently in different situations.

Now fill in how I perceive myself.

Adjective	Description of behaviour

How I believe others perceive me

Adjective	Description of behaviour

Now you can do the behavioural analysis for how you believe others perceive you or how indeed people actually perceive you. If you choose to do this with someone else make sure you feel comfortable and safe with that person.

SUMMARY

What you should have now is your life map, your personal portfolio and a fairly extensive understanding of how you perceive yourself as well as how you believe others perceive you. And if you have been brave you will have information on how others actually perceive you. In addition, you have behavioural evidence as to how you have earned the image you have.

You should now have a full picture of your starting point and the foundation for your journey. The next few chapters will deal with generating the destination of your journey, after which you can start to plot the route you will take to get there.

As part of creating your destination you will need to look at your image again but this time from the perspective of you generating the image you want. You will be in control of your image, not the other way round.

3 Creating Your Desired Image

If you think back to the perception box (how do I perceive myself?) and compare the description there to those in your perception tree, (how I believe others perceive me) you may find there are significant differences.

How do I perceive myself?	How I believe others perceive me

The first issue to explore in your image is the potential difference between how you perceive yourself and how you believe others perceive you (which may also differ from how they actually do see you). In fact, you are probably a bit of both of these and resolving the potential differences is simply the acceptance of what is in both boxes as being valid and ok. You might also like to consider the behavioural evidence you have presented. Is it still current? Is it accurate?

Once you have reconciled these first two sets of perceptions you can move on to dealing with the second issue regarding your image. That is the potential difference between who you are now and who you want to be. Here the plot thickens because there are now four sets of perceptions to think about.

How do I perceive myself?	How I believe others perceive me
How I would like to perceive myself	How I would like others to perceive me

Problems often arise when you think the way the world sees you and the way you would like the world to see you are too far apart. As a result, you end up trying to convey one image of yourself while deep down you may think 'that's not really me'.

In trying to reconcile these differences you end up creating outward images of yourself. You end up not really being who you are, but choosing instead to 'hide' yourself behind masks that portray the image that you wish others to hold of you. These masks protect you from the judgement of others, they hide the truth. This inevitably leads to tension and stress as you constantly try to be this wonderful, perfect person that you think the world expects you to be. The tension increases as the discrepancy between your mask and reality widens.

Understanding your present image is about resolving the differences between the first set of perceptions. Creating and managing your image are about resolving the differences between the second set of perceptions. It is also about making sure that the discrepancies between who you are and who you would like to be are minimal, or at least that you are aware of them, comfortable with them, or working on improving them.

Having done the work on understanding your image, you are now ready to start creating your desired image. To create the image you want is really quite simple. You need to write down the adjectives and phrases that describe the image you desire and write down appropriate patterns of behaviours that would generate that image. Remember to be as consistent as possible between the two boxes shown below.

How I would like to perceive myself	How I would like others to perceive me

YOUR DESIRED IMAGE: THE BEHAVIOURAL ANALYSIS

How I would like to perceive myself	
Adjective	Description of behaviour

How I would like others to perceive me	
Adjective	Description of behaviour

THE BLACKMAILER

You will undoubtedly have some characteristics that you are not so proud of. Being confident about who you are and being able to generate the image you want means you have to accept these somewhat more negative facets of yourself together with all the positive ones.

So far, in reading this book, you have spent the majority of the time looking at all the positive things about yourself. It is time to start looking at those aspects that you are not quite so proud of. After all, if you only looked at the positive, there would be little to improve, and you would not need this book.

Everyone holds some beliefs and information about themselves that they feel the world at large really doesn't need to know about. These beliefs might be based on things you have done or not done. They are often based on your interpretation of events that have happened over the years. They may be general characteristics that you feel are best kept a secret. This part of you is the hidden self and is the part that only you know about.

The hidden self
Information and beliefs about yourself that
you do not normally share with others.

There are also some things that others know, or believe, about you and that you know they know or believe about you. This is common knowledge in that it is shared openly between you and others.

Common knowledge
Information and beliefs that you are
happy to share with other people.

The hidden self
Information and beliefs about yourself that you
do not normally share with other people.

Finally, there are thoughts that others have about you, which you know they have but you don't know what they are. You have a suspicion what the thoughts might be but you have never asked the person concerned to validate your suspicions. These suspicions make up the black-mailer. By suspicions I mean the negative thoughts that you believe others hold about you.

The blackmailer
Information and beliefs that you believe others hold
about you but you have not confirmed your suspicions.

Common knowledge
Information and beliefs that you are
happy to share with other people.

The hidden self
Information and beliefs about yourself that you
do not normally share with other people.

It is your fear or concern of the negative thoughts others might hold about you that provides the blackmailer with a lot of power over you. Your mental blackmailer is very much like a real blackmailer in that you hold beliefs and information about yourself in your 'hidden self' that you believe to be true. In wanting to hide these you provide the blackmailer with an opportunity to discover your secret and hold it against you. I am referring only to your negative self-beliefs, a blackmailer never advertises the good, they are only interested in the bad.

Think back to a time when you made a silly mistake and you were caught. Did you worry about what the other person thought? Or imagine for a moment you are at a party and you have a few too many drinks. You wake up the next morning and think about what you did and said, your next thought is 'oh no'. You worry because you may well have let others see parts of your hidden self and this leaves you feeling a little vulnerable. In fact, your image is at stake.

The reason for this is that you have let someone else see your hidden self and, given that you often do not believe it is a very positive, or good one, you worry because you are afraid you have been found out for who you really are. By showing more of yourself than normal you have in fact decreased your hidden self and put that information into the common knowledge area. This in itself is not a problem, it is only a problem when you start to worry what others think about you. The fear is that by allowing others to see more of who you really are within your hidden self, the more vulnerable you become.

DECREASING YOUR HIDDEN SELF

This is how the blackmailer gets its power, it is your need to hide parts of yourself (your hidden self) that actually makes you vulnerable. For example, as an MSc student I was having great difficulty understanding the lectures for one subject. I struggled on for a while, but eventually came

The blackmailer
Information and beliefs that you believe others hold
about you but you have not confirmed your suspicions.

Common knowledge
Information and beliefs that you are
happy to share with other people.

The hidden self
Information and beliefs about yourself that you
do not normally share.

to the conclusion that my belief about myself, of being a little slow must be true, and that the lecturer also knew that by now. In my hidden self was the belief that I was a little slow, my lack of understanding in the lectures must have been obvious to all, the lecturer certainly must have realized my inadequacy. Believing this to be the case, I was at the mercy of the awesome power of my blackmailer in that I was convinced the lecturer knew my hidden secret and I had been found out for being slow. I worried for several weeks, getting more and more stressed in the lectures till I could hardly keep up with the subject at all. Fortunately, I recognized that the only way to defeat the blackmailer and be free of its crippling hold was to admit my shortcoming, in others words, to talk to the lecturer.

Taking all my courage in hand I went to the lecturer and admitted my secret. I informed the lecturer that I wasn't following all the material and was having serious difficulty understanding more than about 50 per cent of what was being taught. Fearing the worst I waited for his reply. The lecturer smiled and said: 'You're doing quite well then, most people only get about 35 per cent.'

This is a true story of my days at university and, although somewhat simplistic in nature, it does demonstrate the point quite well. In real life, blackmailers lose their power the moment the person being blackmailed is willing to have the secret disclosed publicly. The secrets you hold in your hidden self often do not have all the negative meanings and consequences that you attribute to them.

I am not suggesting that you go out and bare your soul, but just that you recognize that the secrets you feel are so bad perhaps are not all that devastating when they are revealed. Be prepared to have your hidden self discovered. You will find that you lose an enormous fear and are much more able to be yourself and be ok with that. After all, if you really have a look at what is in your hidden self, is it that bad? Moreover, it is probably true to say that everyone has something to hide which means a lot of us share the same fear of disclosing our hidden self. We all end up hiding from each other.

The best way to deal with a blackmailer is to accept yourself, shortcomings and all, to be able to declare openly whatever it is that you think is not good about yourself and what you can do to improve it (you should do this at least to yourself). When you deny it, the blackmailer just gets more power.

> Take away the power of the blackmailer by choosing to allow others to see that you are less than perfect.

After all, when you discover these 'deficiencies' about someone else, don't you feel relieved that they are human after all?

You can also decrease the blackmailer's power by asking people for feedback, by asking them what they think about you. This then increases the common knowledge area by bringing in information and beliefs that others hold about you. The less energy you have to put into protecting your hidden self, the more energy you have for getting on with your life.

DEFEATING THE BLACKMAILER

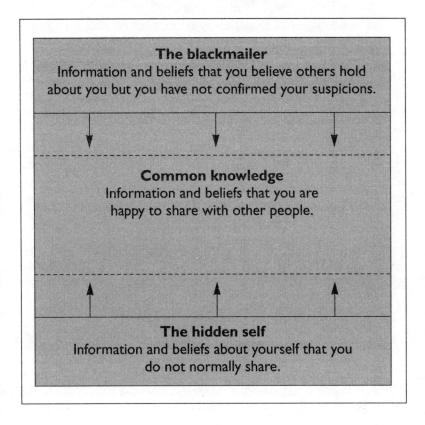

The blackmailer
Information and beliefs that you believe others hold about you but you have not confirmed your suspicions.

Common knowledge
Information and beliefs that you are happy to share with other people.

The hidden self
Information and beliefs about yourself that you do not normally share.

SUMMARY

Most of you probably spend some energy hiding from others this person you know deep inside, because you fear the judgement of other people. It is as if you have an internal blackmailer who has you do all sorts of things just so you are not found out for who you really are. To demonstrate how powerful this can be I would like to share another true story with you. A man was made redundant and rather than admitting this was the case he would leave home every morning as usual and come back in the evening at the same time as he always did when he was working. He used to sit in a park all day. He was unable to tell his wife he had been made redundant because he thought he was not good enough at his job and had been found out.

This story does have a happy ending, he eventually admitted what had happened, was placed on an outplacement programme and got a new job. If he had been able to say what had happened earlier he would have spent much less time sitting in the park feeling miserable.

Your self-image may contain information about the fact that you are not good at something. SO WHAT? Look back at your personal portfolio and your life map, nothing can take away your skills or what you have already achieved. Instead of avoiding fear, face it and do what scares you most.

If you ever feel like you are being a fraud and one day someone is going to find out the truth, your blackmailer is at work.

4 Breaking Through

Toddlers have a great ability to break through barriers that constrain us as adults. They are blissfully unaware of themselves in terms of image, right and wrong. They simply are. Usually the one thing on their mind is their own immediate needs and wants. Then, as they start to grow older and develop their own separate identities, they learn to make sense of their surroundings and to manage their environment. All the signals and messages they receive get interpreted into a sense of the world and their place in it. This is the beginning of the development of their self-image.

There is, however, a small problem here. Think about a young girl standing at the bus stop with her mother. She bends down to do up her shoe lace and as she struggles to make the loops, her mother bends down and says, 'I'll do that.' The mother lightly brushes her child's hands away and does up the shoe laces in a few seconds, just before she lifts the child up and gets on the bus.

There are several possible interpretations of this sequence of events. From the child's point of view it might seem as follows, 'I was doing that; Mummy always does it for me; why can't I do it; I am too slow.' The list can go on. Now think about the mother's perspective. 'There is our bus, we must get on it because we need to get home.' If you have ever seen a child try to do something, only to have an adult intervene and do it for them, the frustration is evident. Learning to eat is always a case in point.

Both perceptions are equally valid but the one the child is likely to hold is not a positive one for themselves. Also given the fact that children start to interpret their environment from an early age they lack some of the objectivity and rationality that we can access as adults. As a result, many of the interpretations you hold of the world, and yourself in it, are based on early learning, learning that is often not correct and hardly ever validated.

For example, imagine you are in a supermarket, you might well witness a child being chastised by a parent for touching the goods, for fidgeting in the trolley, for dropping things, or whatever. Depending on the severity of the parent's reaction you can see children behave in ways that seek reassurance that they are still loved. The parent often has no idea that what the child is going through is a full rejection syndrome. To a child a telling off usually equates to 'not being loved any more'. The parent does not of course equate the telling off with the love they have for the child. The only oversight of the parent is that they forget to let their children know that. So the child remains with its fears and often aggravates the situation by its approval-seeking behaviour, only to throw itself further into the feelings of rejection and the parent into exasperation.

Throughout their early years children experience a myriad of events from which they create interpretations and meanings. Eventually the child makes some conclusions about the world and itself. Then through the principles of generalization the child begins to recognize sequences of events and can predict the consequences of those events before they actually happen.

The process of generalization is very important to the child's learning curve but can also be faulty, especially when they are not validated. The way it works is very simple. For example, a child sees a cat and is told that is a cat. The next day the child sees a dog, realizes it has fur, ears, four legs and a tail and quite logically says 'cat'. The parents smile at each other and correct the child, saying, 'No, that's a dog because it is bigger.' The next day the family take a trip to the country where the child sees a cow.

The child thinks here is a four-legged animal with fur, ears, four legs, a tail and it is bigger than a cat, and excitedly shouts: 'dog, dog'. The parents explain that this is not a dog but a cow because it is even bigger than a dog. So on and on, until the child has learnt enough discriminators to be able to classify all animate and inanimate objects correctly.

However, when it comes to classifying sequences of events and their associated feelings, not only does the child not have the language to be able to express itself clearly but I suspect that most adults would have difficulty as well. The child simply learns that a certain sequence of events will lead to certain feelings. For example, getting dressed up in your Sunday best means adults pat you on the head, smile and talk about you as if you aren't in the room. Doing exams usually means parents get nervous when the results are due to come through.

Events occur and these carry consequences, dropping the milk bottle (event) incurs mother's anger and induces shouting, etc (consequence). This makes the child feel that the milk bottle is more important, that they have done something really bad and that they are no good (interpretation). Their next thought might go as follows, 'I must be clumsy', or 'don't do things because if it goes wrong you're in trouble', etc (conclusion). This perhaps is a somewhat dramatic example but it demonstrates the generation of beliefs you hold about yourself. They are rooted in events and your conclusions of how those events made you feel at the time. Given that these started with your young mind they are often over-simplistic interpretations of your world. Several similar interpretations and conclusions lead to beliefs.

Once a belief has taken hold you look for evidence to verify it.

Next time that child tries something and gets it wrong, mother reacts in a similar way; the conclusion that they get it wrong is reinforced and the belief strengthened. Again, the message they learn is: do not try to do things because you will get it wrong and that hurts.

By now you may well be thinking of your own events, interpretations and stories. Below is some space to jot down any thoughts you may be having.

```
My thoughts



```

Slowly some basic beliefs about yourself are built up with what you feel is good solid evidence. Once the belief is established, all contrary evidence is selectively ignored in favour of supporting evidence. It's a bit like having a jury that has already made up its mind. Each event is no longer examined on its own merit, but it is placed under the scrutiny of previous evidence, conclusions and beliefs. If it fits then it must be correct. If it doesn't then it is simply ignored.

Fear of presentations is a good example of this principle at work. Often your first presentation is not so good, and you feel like a failure or are embarrassed by your inability to get your point across. Or worse, you leave the podium before getting through to the end. Your conclusion is that you aren't any good at presentations. If you ever try it again, you first relive the nightmare of the first experience and are sure you will go through the same thing again. Of course as you get more practice you get better and your presentations improve. However, it takes many good presentations to undo the upset of your first bad one. Surely this is illogical. If the cold evidence shows that you have done five acceptable presentations and one bad one, your conclusion must be that you can give acceptable or even good presentations. However, that doesn't fit into your beliefs and therefore it simply gets ignored as evidence. As a result, you keep reliving the anguish of doing bad presentations. We need to consciously counteract faulty evidence and conclusions and learn to look at the objective facts.

The conclusions you make lead you to behave in certain ways. In the example above, after giving your first presentation you may spend the rest of your life avoiding giving them because you don't like the feeling that goes with it. Depending on what conclusion you have made about yourself, you generate appropriate behaviour patterns to protect yourself from those hurtful feelings. Initially they are good survival and coping mechanisms, but there comes a time when you need to reassess your evidence and throw out the biased jury for an objective one.

Many people live with fears that they have generated a long time ago only to find that when they finally face this fear, actually there was nothing to be afraid of. You may like to take a few minutes here to think about times when you have been afraid of something only to find that when you were thrust into that situation you could handle it relatively easily.

CORE BELIEFS

What is it in your being that always has you question yourself? You are probably your own hardest critic. Now why is that? Are you born that way or is it a skill you learn? This is where I can hear you saying that it depends on personality, on upbringing, on your whole past experience and you might well be right. All this is true but that doesn't mean you can't change it as an adult.

Clearly the crucial factor is your perception of yourself, your levels of self-recognition and confidence. Your self-image depends not only on what you have been through in your life but also how you experienced and interpreted these events. This is where the problem starts, with your interpretation of events and things that happen to you. You start developing interpretations in early childhood but unfortunately don't have the intellectual capacity to rationalize events. As a child you work on feelings not facts.

All this, of course, is not new, but it can solve some of your basic insecurities about yourself. Think about something that you know you're not good at. Now think about how you came to that conclusion, and when you came to that conclusion. The likely answers to these questions are that either you attempted something and failed, someone told you that you were no good at it, or someone laughed at your attempt.

When you learnt to speak as a child, didn't you make mistakes? And didn't people laugh? Still you learnt to speak, you didn't stop trying just because it was hard. And yet that is exactly what you do as an adult. You stop trying, you stop believing in yourself. Do you remember saying to yourself as a child, I will never learn to speak so what's the point? Imagine as a child you take your first tentative steps and fall. You didn't sit there and say, 'Well, I looked really silly doing that I am not going to do it again.' No, of course not. As a baby you are blissfully unaware of yourself as a separate entity. Just as well really.

This all changes, as you grow older, you become aware of yourself in your environment, you literally become self-conscious. You start to worry about how you appear to others. For example, there is someone you really like and you want a relationship with him or her, but the story in your head goes something like this 'I can't go out with him because I always mess up relationships, I can't give commitment, or they always leave me. I know this is going to leave me vulnerable and hurt, so why go through all the pain? I'd better not call him because it is always the same and he would probably reject me anyway.'

As a child you build your perception of the world and yourself in it and create survival mechanisms. You learn which actions or set of circumstances bring you pain and which bring you pleasure. You learn not to do things that bring pain and to do things that bring pleasure or pay-off. You create patterns of behaviour which ensure your survival and at the time they really work, they are what gets you through life. Some of these are very powerful and positive. However, some become inappropriate as you grow up, they become out of date and are a reaction to your view of the world rather than a real danger. An example of this is when a child feels that its parents aren't there for its protection and the people in the world are not to be trusted. The child will start to rely on itself for its safety. As they grow up, these children collect their evidence and become more and more independent. They feel they don't need anybody, they can manage everything by themselves. Initially, this may have been a good survival mechanism, but as they grow older it prevents them from creating relationships. After all, they don't need anybody, and anyway if they did admit they needed someone they might get hurt because people aren't to be trusted.

To avoid the pain of being let down or betrayed, the child doesn't look to anyone other than itself for safety. This may work in many positive ways but there are also costs. Everything you do has a cost and a pay-off. The pay-off here is that the person is self-reliant, the cost is that it is hard for them to admit that they need other people and with that comes the difficulty of maintaining relationships.

The event cycle in Figure 4.1 shows how your interpretations of, and conclusions about, the events in your lives lead to actions, which have results or consequences. Your actions comprise behaviours that carry with them a pay-off, something you get out of it and a cost, something you lose. Each action has a pay-off and a cost, for example, being distant with people might be a way of protecting yourself from being vulnerable (pay-off). However, this same behaviour alienates people and makes relationship building difficult (cost).

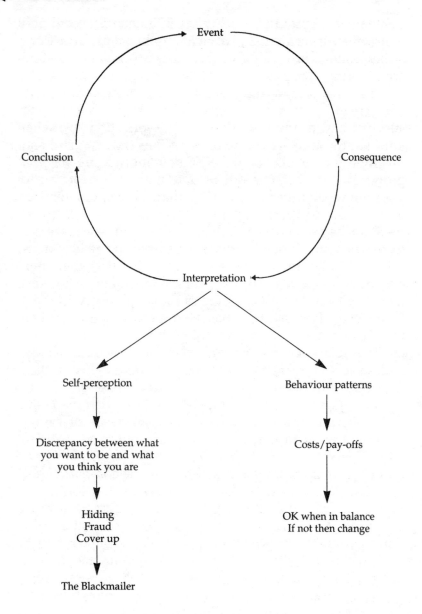

Figure 4.1 *The event cycle*

As long as the pay-off of an action is greater than the cost, you will maintain that behaviour. As soon as the cost becomes too high, you will seek to establish a new behaviour with a higher pay-off.

This concept may feel somewhat cold and alien. It is not intended to be. You are rarely totally conscious of the pay-offs and costs of your behaviour. Often you do not take the time to question them or the assumptions they are based on.

When the balance of cost and pay-off changes and you recognize it, you are forced to change. You are forced to create new possibilities, interpretations and perhaps even renew your self-perceptions.

The conclusions you draw as a result of the actions and their consequences are the basis of your self-perceptions. When there is a discrepancy between what you want to be and what you think you are, you start to generate patterns of behaviour that will cover up that discrepancy, and that's when the blackmailer can take charge.

INTERPRETATIONS

As an adult you need to learn to manage your negative beliefs and feelings, you need to become an objective scientist and an evidence collector. This needs to be done at a conscious level. The easiest way to start is by looking at events that have occurred and how they made you feel. Very much like when one starts a diet: the advice is to start by monitoring everything you eat each day. This provides invaluable evidence about what is happening. Only then can appropriate action be planned accordingly. Start managing your beliefs by writing down key events that occur each day. This should take just a couple of minutes each evening.

For example, let's say you are happily driving along and someone cuts across you to turn without any warning or regard for your safety. How would you describe that event? Or you have been waiting patiently in a queue and someone jumps in ahead of you. How would you feel?

When something happens, feelings are generated by the associated meaning that you attribute to the event. Mostly, however, you don't analyse the meaning at the time: you simply feel and react. So the event creates a feeling, which is generated by the meaning you have attributed to the event. Similar events will generate similar feelings because the underlying meaning you attribute to them is the same. That is why in certain situations you always get angry, frustrated or intimidated. It's like a trigger that always gets a similar reaction. You might even go as far as allowing people that remind you of someone to influence how you feel about them.

When you first meet somebody new you have an opinion about them within about seven seconds and, what's more, you assume that you are correct. The question is, what do you base that opinion on? Anyway, the point here is that you attribute meanings to events which then generate a feeling.

Using either the information you have been gathering over the past week or alternatively just thinking about recent events, simply write down the event and the feeling that went with it. Choose events that made you feel angry, embarrassed, uncomfortable or gave you any other negative feeling.

Event	Feeling
The tap broke again	Anger and frustration
My partner was very grumpy after work	Tired, curious and helpless
Someone in a shop was rude to me	Indignation, anger

Collecting your evidence: monitoring

Event	Feeling

After a few days of acknowledging events and how you feel about them you will learn to listen to your feelings rather than simply react to them. They will start to become conscious. This is, however, only the first step towards learning how to manage the natural triggers that you have. The next step is somewhat more difficult because it needs you to suspend your feelings and to analyse the meaning.

Event	Feeling	Meaning
The tap broke again	Anger and frustration	I paid to have it fixed, it will waste more of my time, I will have a fight with the plumber, why can't anyone get things right, he's making a fool of me, I am stupid, I am dependent on him because I don't know how to fix it, I am useless.

As you can see, a simple event like a broken tap can have a whole range of meanings to it. Can you see what has happened? The event means something. The point is that it really doesn't matter what the events are. Their meaning becomes all important and the meaning is what will generate a feeling and subsequently your response.

The event in the example above may have any or all of the meanings attached to it. However, there is probably one that is really significant. When the implications or the meaning comes close to a negative belief we hold about ourselves, the blackmailer comes into action. You feel threatened because part of your hidden self is about to be, or has been, exposed. It is at this time that you get triggered by the feeling which becomes all powerful and drives your action at that moment. Perhaps you experience sudden anger, fear or stress.

In the case above the significant meanings might be 'he's making a fool of me' and 'I am useless'. So the fact that the tap broke has made the person feel silly and useless. No wonder there are some feelings attached to the event!

A common event that many people get very upset about is being kept waiting. Let's talk it through. The event: you had an appointment, the other person is late and you are waiting. How many times do you find your levels of irritation increase the longer you wait? Now ask yourself why that is? All that is happening is that you are waiting but your anger just keeps getting stronger and stronger. Finally they arrive and the first thing you say with a tone of frustration is 'You're late.' So the feeling is one of anger, frustration, being let down or something similar. What is the meaning?

We usually make it mean; 'I'm not important enough for them to be on time and keep their commitment to me, there was something or someone else more important, I was here on time, I made the effort, they don't respect me, they feel more important than me, they are wasting my time, and so on.' In the business world, keeping people waiting is sometimes used to intimidate and give *exactly* these messages and most of the time people fall for it.

Having realized how meanings and feelings are attached to events, your attention must focus on how you can own those feelings and meanings and take control of them. The concept is very simple. You have a choice, the feelings rule you or you rule the feelings. That doesn't mean that you have to become a cold and unfeeling person. The feelings will still occur but you will gain the ability to choose how you react to them.

Imagine you are walking down the street and there is a small group of people walking towards you. They are looking at you and saying something and then there's a giggle. Wouldn't you wonder what they had said about you? Maybe they weren't speaking about you at all. It's an assumption you make. I know you feel pretty sure about your conclusions but unless you validate them you can't prove it to be correct or incorrect.

I could go on citing hundreds of examples of people getting upset by a sequence of events because of the meaning that they have attributed to those events, all based on assumptions. The events may or may not mean what you've made them mean. The question is, why do you believe the meanings you attribute to events? You rarely have proof for them. You rarely ask people to verify your interpretation. When was the last time that someone was late for their appointment with you and you asked them 'Are you late because I'm not important enough for you to be on time?'

Now take your event and feeling list and take a few minutes by yourself to be honest and write down what the events mean to you. To help identify the meaning ask yourself the following questions. What does the event imply about me? Or what does the event show about how others perceive me?

Your evidence to meaning: interpretations

Event	Feeling	Meaning

The tricky bit comes next, if the meaning is positive and makes you feel good. Fine, leave it alone. If, however, the meaning gives you a negative, angry, upset or worried feeling then question your assumptions.

The fact is, you make assumptions and then believe your own interpretations. Why should you, especially when they make you feel bad? Go back and look at some of the meanings. Now prove them to be right. Provide objective evidence that proves your meaning beyond any doubt. Impossible, isn't it? Now you are ready to start to manage your interpretations, and thereby your conclusions and beliefs, not to mention your feelings. Try to generate alternative meanings. In the example of the broken tap, alternative meanings might be that, he (the plumber) had a bad day, he is incompetent, he has too much work and is stressed, the parts he replaced are faulty (something he could not have known), or perhaps it is not the same problem.

Any of the new meanings listed above are just as valid as the original list. There is, however, one huge difference and that is in the feelings they generate. Make sure you spend adequate time with your list to generate alternative meanings. Then ask yourself which set of meanings gives you the better feeling. Probably the second list. Since neither set of meanings are proven to be correct or incorrect, why not choose the ones that make you feel better? Now choose which feelings you want and therefore which interpretation you choose to believe. Remember: you don't usually check your interpretations, they are all equally valid. So why choose the one that makes you feel bad?

Have you ever had a conversation with a person who said or did something that you didn't quite understand? Later you think long and hard about what it really was they were trying to convey. You start dragging in all sorts of pieces of information about them, yourself and the exchange that will help you to interpret the event and make sense out of it. You search for the meaning. Sometimes it's the things that aren't said that generate all this analysis in you. Well, unless you're prepared to go and ask the person concerned exactly what they meant, you could try to guess the meaning forever and never be sure.

The problem is that we live by these meanings as if they are true and most of the time they are negative. My challenge to you is to start seeing the events in their objective light, to experience whatever feeling they give you without reacting immediately, to search for the meaning you have given them and finally, to create and choose the meaning that leaves you with the best possible feeling. Then you can take action.

The meanings you assume to be right are the ones that will fit into your assumptions and beliefs of the world. All other alternative meanings may seem illogical because they do not fit your past evidence. That's fine except that who says that your perception of the world was right in the first place?

Here's an example from a client of mine (I'll call him John). John was made redundant. His story: 'My boss [Sarah] made me redundant. I don't understand it, my appraisal was really good and I get on really well with Sarah. I was her best team member, so why did she make me redundant? She's been using me all these years and now I am dispensable. My work isn't acknowledged, and she has been lying to me.'

This clearly is a negative story and not a very powerful one for creating a new future. After talking to John for a while, I found out that Sarah had had a strong disagreement with her boss [Tony]. I proposed the following positive interpretation. Tony wanted to harm Sarah as much as possible so he took out the best team member (John), pulled rank to do it and, in one fell swoop, weakened Sarah's team and therefore her ability to meet her targets.

This alternative story was never proven but it sounded plausible and gave John a different perspective on his redundancy and a much more positive outlook on his own abilities and his future.

Your beliefs, assumptions and interpretations about events are based on your self-perceptions and your perceptions of the world. Most of these can be traced back to a few core beliefs and, in my experience as a coach, most of us have at least one of the following core beliefs.

Core belief	Needs of people holding these core beliefs
I am a failure	These people need to be seen to be succeeding
I am a fraud	These people spend a lot of time hiding in case they are found out
I am not good enough	These people need to be seen to be better than most and to be right
I am not loveable	These people will go to extraordinary lengths to be seen to be loved, they have difficulty saying no to requests that are made of them
I am stupid	These people need to be seen to be intelligent, intellectual, smart
I am not likeable	These people need to be liked and will often pay a huge price to avoid conflict

What beliefs do you think you hold? Remember your core beliefs can generate very positive behaviours as well. Each has its pay-offs and costs. Beliefs like 'I am a failure' can actually be very positive because you might work very hard to disprove it so you end up succeeding.

Is the core belief running you or are you running it?

If you have difficulty seeing at least one of your core beliefs, look back through your event, feeling and meaning exercise and see if there are any trends or similarities in the events that made you angry or upset. Keep asking the question: what does that mean about me?

Fear of failure. How many of you can identify with this? It is probably the most common fear. 'If I do this will I succeed? What if I get it wrong? Will I fall flat on my face? Will I look silly? What will people think?' All these good reasons can spring to mind as to why you shouldn't take the risks that need to be taken. You can usually think of hundreds of reasons why something probably wouldn't be a good idea.

Fear of failing can have a paralysing effect. 'If I try I might fail, so I won't try anything that I don't already know I can do.' Consider the following.

Failure = not achieving your goal

Not doing anything = not achieving your goal

So not doing anything = failure

We all make mistakes and it's ok to make mistakes. It's the only way you can learn. If you do not know what doesn't work, how can you find out what does? Every mistake is an opportunity for learning, each mistake tells you something about how *not* to do things. It is only by trying out new things that any discoveries are made and naturally some of the new things you do will go wrong.

SUMMARY

Remember that your interpretation of events may not be correct. Interpretations are tricky things and unless you ask someone directly what they think and feel, you had better not make any guesses because the chances are you will be incorrect and these interpretations will have a negative impact on you.

If you have not checked your interpretation and it is a negative one, then dump the interpretation. You have the responsibility to yourself to choose how you feel about things. Also you have the responsibility to choose how you interpret things. You need to stick to the facts. Since you cannot prove the interpretation why choose to live with a negative one?

Also, ask yourself: is it better not to try anything in case it goes wrong or is it better to try something new that may yield wonderful results? The question is about the risk you are prepared to take.

5 Taking Back Your Power

Being powerful in life is understanding that either life drives you or you drive it. It is true many events happen over which you have no control. However, you still have control over how you feel about them and what you do about them. The concept here is one of understanding that you have choices and that, having made choices, you are responsible for the resulting consequences.

In other words, taking back your power is understanding your choices and accepting responsibility for the consequences of these choices. Even when you feel you had little choice about the consequences, you can still choose how you feel about them and, therefore, how you manage them. Everything you do, or fail to do, carries consequences with it. You own all those consequences.

This chapter will explore how you can take responsibility for the events in your life and their consequences. It is about seeing that blame and complaining are sure ways of handing over all your power either to someone else or to the situation.

Imagine that you have had a strong disagreement with someone. You can choose several courses of action. You can ignore them and the problem, you can wait for them to come to you in an attempt to resolve the issue, or you can go to them in an attempt to resolve it.

Choosing to ignore it will leave the situation incomplete. Waiting for them to resolve the situation leaves you at their mercy. The third option shows you are able to take responsibility for what has happened and are able to do something about it.

RIGHT VERSUS WRONG

Being able to take action to resolve the situation requires that you are able to sit back, do your event, feeling and meaning exercise and forget about what may be right or wrong. Worrying about being right or being wrong, strong or weak, does nothing to resolve the situation. Even if you are right, so what? The situation is still the same. Whichever course of action you choose you should rejoice in the consequence, as you are the one who has chosen it. Taking responsibility is realizing that the only person who can do anything about the situation in your life is you. If you wait for others it could take a very long time.

There are basically three approaches you can take to dealing with events in your life.

- The passive approach: I'm wrong and you're right, let's do it your way.
- The aggressive approach: I'm right and you're wrong, let's do it my way.
- The assertive approach: I'm right and you're right, let's work on it together.

In taking responsibility it is crucial that you think and plan the strategy you will adopt. For example, if you choose to take responsibility for managing your relationships, you need to give careful thought as to how you approach the person involved. You may feel that you are not angry or blaming them. However, if there is anything in your verbal or body language that suggests to them that you feel you are right, you may as well not have the conversation at all.

If in doubt about where to start, always use questions, avoid statements. Adopt an inquisitorial approach. Think about when someone has approached you with an accusing tone or stance as opposed to someone approaching you with curiosity and a desire to understand. Your behaviour is likely to be very different in each of these cases.

PERSPECTIVE TAKING

You react to events and events react to you. Changing something you do will change the reaction you get or the situation you are in. One of the easiest things to change is how you see a situation, in other words, your perspective. All this takes is looking at the situation from how others might see it. Imagine different people you know and think about what they would say about the situation or how they might see it.

The technique for achieving an assertive approach is to see the situation from the other's perspective. If you and I are looking at the same object from different angles we will see different things. Your description of the object will be different from mine and both will be right. Similarly, two people may go and see the same film and come out with very different perceptions of it. Which one is right? Even two people in verbal communication together can walk away from the exchange with very different ideas of what was said and agreed. Which one is right? In all these examples both views are right, they are just different.

Whether you feel you are more a passive or an aggressive type of person, just try to say to yourself that all perspectives are valid and legitimate. There is no wrong or right and there is no better or worse. There are, of course, a few universally agreed rights and wrongs like the taking of life or the violation of human rights. You will all have a few of these that make up your values in life. But they are probably few.

COMPLETING THE PAST

For most people there are situations where they have been hurt, betrayed, let down or something equivalent. These things happen, it is how you deal with them that is important. Leaving the situation undealt with leaves it incomplete, something for your mind to carry around. It also means that similar events will trigger a whole set of emotions that are not necessarily related to the present but may bring up the past as well.

By the time most people are thirty they have a suitcase full of events and upsets that they carry with them. The difficulty is that, as the suitcase gets fuller, it gets heavier and it takes more and more of your energy to carry around, leaving less and less energy to do something positive and powerful. It is essential that you keep the suitcase as light as you can. Remember earlier in the book the idea of asking people directly for their opinions about you? This is aimed at preventing the blackmailer getting hold of you but also it prevents things being packed into your suitcase. Once everything has been fully discussed and understood, there is nothing for you to put in your suitcase.

So how do you complete the past? Well, the first step is to stop worrying about right and wrong. You may well feel that it is important for the other person to acknowledge they are wrong about something. If that is what you feel, then you are not ready to deal with the situation. You are ready to be right which is very different. Apart from a few absolutes, right and wrong is fairly relative, it all depends on how you see the situation. Remember: the moment you think you are right you have made someone else wrong. How much do you enjoy being wrong? Well, the other person probably feels the same way about it.

When you are ready to approach the situation with an open mind, and can take an assertive approach, the next step is to have a look in your suitcase and see which relationships or people you keep in there. Perhaps somebody did something that you find unforgivable, or something that still gets you angry just thinking about it or the person involved. Or perhaps you told someone a small lie and the relationship has never been quite the same since. Think of a situation where you blame something or someone for the consequences you had to put up with. Now follow these steps.

Completion requires the following, as shown in Figure 5.1.

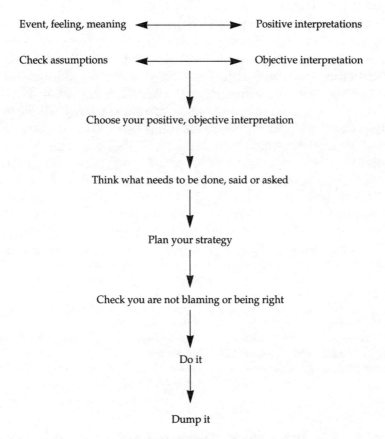

Figure 5.1 *Completing the past*

PAY-OFF AND THE COSTS OF ACTIONS

Sometimes it is very hard to see what you can do to change things. You might think that you have tried everything. Well, the simple rule is that if you are trying something and it isn't getting the desired results, then clearly you are not doing the right thing. Try anything else because if you keep doing what you're doing, you're going to keep getting what you're getting.

However, it is not quite that simple because your behaviour, as has been mentioned earlier, has a pay-off and a cost. You need to stop and think about what these might be before you will able to change your behaviour. For example, imagine a house with two students living in it, Simon and Paul. They have agreed that they will all clean the house on Saturdays and each has been assigned certain tasks. Over the weeks Simon consistently breaks the agreement. Paul, of course, is getting more and more angry each week until finally he does Simon's tasks as well as his own. Paul feels he has tried to talk to Simon but it just wasn't getting him anywhere. When Simon sees Paul doing the work he suddenly offers to do it but Paul refuses the offer and continues to clean the house by himself. Looking at Paul's behaviour there are some clear pay-offs and costs.

Pay-off of Paul's behaviour	Costs of Paul's behaviour
Paul gets to be indignant and make Simon feel wrong for not keeping to the agreement	Paul has to clean the house by himself He is risking his relationship with Simon

In order for Paul to be able to change his behaviour and the situation he will first need to recognize his pay-offs and costs and then create a new behaviour pattern with a different set of pay-offs and costs. He will only change his behaviour when the new pay-offs are more attractive than the old ones or if the new costs are less than the old ones.

When trying to change your behaviour do a quick analysis using the following matrix, it will help you identify why you might want to change your behaviour in the first place.

Pay-off and cost analysis

Pay-off of current behaviour	Cost of current behaviour
Pay-off of new behaviour	Cost of new behaviour

In the example above Paul might change his behaviour by talking the situation through with Simon and trying to resolve it. The pay-off of this new behaviour might be that he improves his relationship with Simon but the cost is that he will have to give up feeling wronged and learn to understand where Simon is coming from. There may even be a cost to having the conversation with Simon in that it might lead to conflict.

WORST-CASE SCENARIOS

Let's say that in your company there have been a number of redundancies recently and everyone is on edge thinking – am I next? Everyone, including you, is extra careful not to attract too much attention, and everyone is more fearful than usual of making mistakes as it might be used as an excuse to make them redundant. Then things start to go wrong. You make a mistake and worry so much about it that you lose concentration and make another. In your mind you can see how your future will look. Your mind keeps going over and over these future events till you feel as though you have already been made redundant.

Your fear of redundancy becomes paralysing and you are bound on this course of events waiting for the inevitable. The fear is mounting, the stress levels are increasing, your home life is deteriorating and you can do nothing except watch yourself approach redundancy.

Two things. One, your assumptions will have you behave in a way that will make them true because that's the evidence you are looking for and you usually find it because you are normally right. Two, your behaviour, body language, tone, everything you do in communication will elicit the response you expect.

You map out in your mind the course of events and then watch it happen. Now just stop there for a minute because what would happen if you challenged your assumptions and mapped out a different course of events? You may still feel that one is more likely to happen but at least there is an alternative. Figure 5.2 shows an event chain.

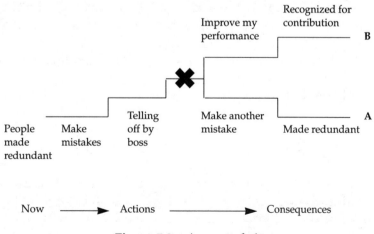

Figure 5.2 *An event chain*

Every chain of events has choices along it. You need to alter your view of the future events if you are to change your future. Such a choice point is shown by ✖ on the event chain in Figure 5.2. At these points you need to examine your imagined event chains and change them. You need to avoid the negative self-fulfilling prophecy and replace it with a positive one. For example, 'I will improve my performance such that I get recognition for it.'

Step one of the process is to walk through the events mentally and see whether there is anything you can do to change the course of events to have consequence 'B' which is that you do not lose your job but instead get acknowledgement for your performance. This means believing that you are in charge and able to create the consequences that you want. In order to do that you need to know what you want. You need to be able to imagine that as vividly as you can the negative scenario and then you need to work towards it.

Step two is to stand back and acknowledge that 'A' is a real possibility but, rather than wait for it to happen, you could plan for dealing with the consequence when it does. So you might start looking in the paper for a new job, or exploring how to manage your finance better. You need to consider all possible actions that you would take should 'A' happen. Generate an action plan for the event so that if it happens you are prepared. Most fears are about things that haven't happened yet and about not knowing how to deal with them if they do. If you are prepared for it, then your fear levels will become more rational and easier to deal with.

Another example, one that is simpler and uses the same principle. Imagine you have been invited to a dinner party. You know it is going to be an awful experience. You nevertheless go and indeed it is an awful experience. Most likely, it was your attitude and nothing else that made it an awful experience (if any of you at this point are saying no, it was awful because ... then go back and reread the last few pages about owning the consequences of your actions).

To take ownership of your life means you get to create

what you want. That means you have to be able to see what is possible for you, you need to be able to dream and hold a vision of yourself and your life that for you is powerful, fun, and fulfilling. The next chapter will look at how you can do that.

There are of course times when negative interpretations or consequences are real and will happen. For these occasions remember the fear of it happening is what is paralysing. Once the event has occurred you are forced to act. It is often the fact that we do not know how we should behave or what we should do in the feared consequence that keeps that fear alive. If redundancy is a real possibility then you must start to plan for it perhaps by writing your CV, hunting for jobs, saving money, checking your legal rights etc. Planning for prevention of the consequence and planning for the consequence can both help to reduce fear.

SUMMARY

The only way to have a choice in your life is to own the consequences of your actions, you can own or disown your life depending on how you deal with events in it. How often do you blame others or circumstances for your problems and upsets? It's much easier to say, 'I couldn't get the report out because I was still waiting for information from the finance department.'

In relationships this is often the cause of breakdown because each partner accuses the other of doing or not doing something that has caused the problem in the relationship. When you blame others or external events for your emotions or inability to do something, you in fact give away ALL your power to do anything to change the situation. After all, if it isn't your fault why should you do anything? Or, indeed, what can you do?

Well, the truth is that, in blaming, you are handing your life over to others or to the circumstances. The question to ask yourself is: what can I do to change things? You might like to make a few notes here.

6 Generating Your Future

If you were making a journey from your house to a friend's house you would need to know where your house is in relation to theirs. You would need to know where your journey starts and where it ends. Look at your life as a journey. If you want to get anywhere you need to know where you are starting from and where you intend to go. Without these two reference points you will simply get lost, end up in a place where you don't want to be, or take twice as long to get there.

In this chapter you are not concerned with how you make the journey. That will be covered in the following chapter. Rather, the point of this chapter is to imagine where your journey will take you. All you are concerned with here is, where do you want to go?

The difficulty is that often you are so sure of what you can and cannot do that when you try to create a vision for yourself, all you can see are the problems and obstacles that stand in your way. Think about the following areas in your life, and any others you feel I have omitted, and dream of how you would like your life to be.

Family	Friends	Work	Health
Love	Integrity	Money	Relationships
Communication	Sex and intimacy	Values	Support

CREATING A VISION DRAWING

Creating a vision is about mentally putting yourself in the future and looking around you to see what you have in your life at that point in time. Think about everything you would like to have in your life and simply draw a picture of it. Don't worry about your ability to draw: that is not the object of the exercise. Your brain thinks faster than you can articulate the thoughts, so drawing is the quickest way to translate your ideas into something more tangible.

For example, a vision might be, maintain my relationship with my partner, engage in plenty of sports, own a house, have a successful business, and write a book. This vision drawing is shown in Figure 6.1.

Figure 6.1 *A vision drawing*

Now draw your vision for the future.

MIND MAPPING

The next thing to do is to look at the priorities and dependencies. For this, mind mapping can be useful. Start with the key elements of your vision and simply allow your brain free thought and note these thoughts with their natural links. Going back to the example of my vision drawing I would use the house, the book, sports, a successful business and my partner as starting points. The thought of a house might bring to mind the mortgage or the journey to work

An example of an initial mind map is shown in Figure 6.2.

Once you have drawn your initial mind map, expand the links between the bubbles to make a complete mind map. Be as creative as you like. Figure 6.3 shows my expanded complete mind map.

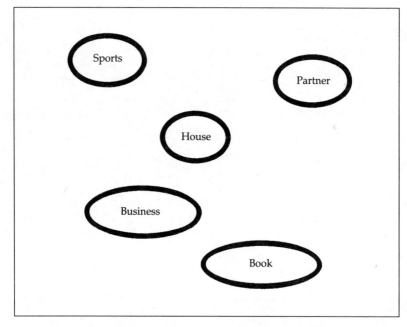

Figure 6.2 *An initial mind map*

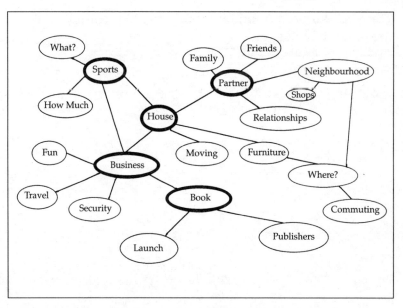

Figure 6.3   *A complete mind map*

Now draw the initial elements of your own mind map.

Now expand your initial mind map to complete it by drawing the links.

CONDITIONS OF SATISFACTION

Once you have thought through your vision, and made a mind map, you are ready to get specific about what exactly do these things look like in reality. You need to generate clear conditions of satisfaction, tangible evidence that you have achieved the elements of your vision and mind map.

As you work on your mind map or conditions of satisfaction, your thoughts will become more and more defined. In the example below, the key element of the house becomes more defined to that of 'security' which incorporates the house as well as a car and a satisfactory income.

What do I want?	How will I know I've got it?
Strong relationship	Sharing activities with my partner
Security	House Car Savings of £10,000 in the bank Income of £30,000
Business	A team of 20 £50,000 cash in the bank
Sports	Play tennis twice a week, in top ten of the club league
Book	Sell 2,000 copies of my book

Now fill in your conditions of satisfaction.

What do I want?	How will I know I've got it?

SUMMARY

After reading this chapter you should be feeling quite excited, you have now created your vision, your mind map to show the elements and their links, as well as clear conditions you would have in your life when you achieve your vision. Put all the questions of how you can do this aside for a moment. That will become apparent in the next chapter. If what you have in front of you at this moment is not inspiring you, I recommend you revisit this chapter and think bigger or differently. At this point you may well be feeling a little apprehensive and wondering how you will achieve your vision. Read on to find out.

7 Translating the Dream into Reality

There is only one person who can decide to make your vision come true and make it happen. That person, of course, is you. At the beginning of the book you spent quite some time looking at where you are, your image and your blackmailer. Having decided where you are and through visioning and mind mapping where you want to be, you can now plan your journey from one to the other.

The process is always the same:

Where am I now?	– Describe the situation as it is.
Where do I want to be?	– Imagine the situation as you would like it to be.
How do I get there?	– What can I do to have things the way I want them?
	– What are the steps I would have to take?
	– Do I commit myself to taking the required action and making the required changes?
Take the first step	– DO IT NOW!

The first step is often the hardest but all it takes is a commitment from you.

MAKING SENSE OF COMPLEXITY

Using a simple technique called affinity mapping you can translate all your ideas from the vision and mind map into a logical action plan that will achieve your conditions of satisfaction.

To create your affinity map take your vision and your mind map and brainstorm any actions you can see will need to be done. Record each action as a verb onto a card or 'Post-it' note and randomly lay these on a table. Now simply sort them into groups that naturally link together. Don't think too hard. Just use your intuition to put the cards in groups that seem similar or have an affinity for each other. Your mind map should suggest some natural affinities. An example of an affinity map is shown in Figure 7.1.

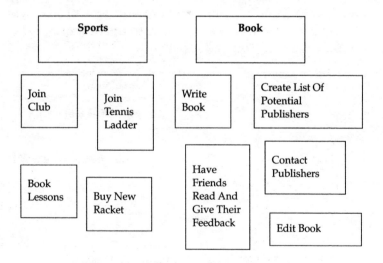

Figure 7.1 *An affinity map*

Using natural resources

The next step in creating your action plan is to consider opportunities that may prevent or help you achieve your vision. This can be done in three stages, first think about the strengths you have that will help you to achieve your actions plan, then think about existing circumstances or opportunities that you can access to support you. Finally write down the actions you would need to take to maximize these strengths and opportunities.

Strengths I can use to get what I want	Actions to use strengths
Book – My friends and acquaintances	They already know some publishers
Sports – I am fit	Join the club ladder at a higher level
Opportunities that exist	Actions to use opportunities
Sports – Some friends are members already	Visit different clubs to find right one
Sports – Two friends are members of a club	Perhaps they would provide the necessary references for membership application

As you can see, some specific actions come out of this exercise, for example:

1. Book – Contact my friends and acquaintances.
2. Sports – Ask friends to be able to visit clubs.
3. Sports – Choose the right club (private or public).
4. Sports – Ask for support on membership application.

Write down all your new actions on separate Post-it notes and add them to your affinity map.

PLANNING FOR MAXIMUM POTENTIAL

As with natural resources, you also need to consider anything that might stand in the way of you achieving what you want in your vision. You will need to think about your weaknesses and about any threats that will prevent you from achieving your vision, then write down the actions you can take to circumvent these. Here is an example of planning for maximum potential.

My weaknesses	Actions to overcome weaknesses
Sports – Lack of time	Plan ahead, set time aside in diary make commitments to friends and tennis coach
What threats and obstacles are there?	Actions to minimize threats

Similarly, some clear actions come out of this exercise. These will help prevent obstacles becoming problems.

1. Sports – Make commitments to friends
2. Sports – Create budget
3. Sports – Create savings plan
4. Sports – Book lesson in advance

Write down all your new actions on separate Post-it notes and add them to your affinity map. Figure 7.2 shows an affinity map in its unordered state.

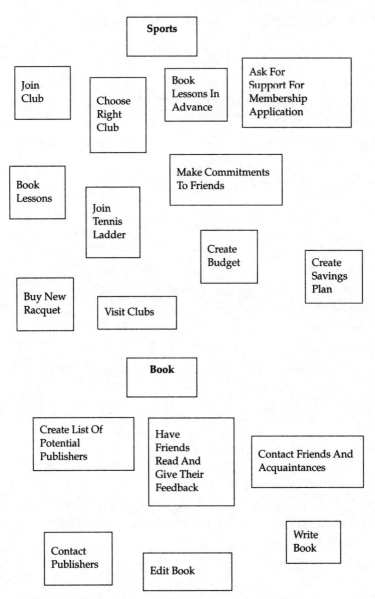

Figure 7.2 *Unordered affinity map*

Ordered affinity map

Keep shuffling the cards or Post-its around until you feel comfortable that each group represents a set of actions that go together and that will complete a step towards your vision. Finally place the cards or Post-its in their natural time order as shown in Figure 7.3 for Sports.

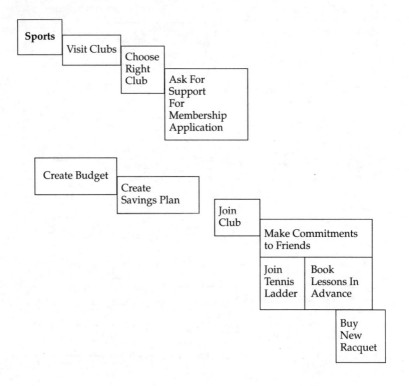

Figure 7.3 *Affinity map in time order: Sports*

Some actions can be done at the same time. In the example above I can start to visit clubs at the same time as creating a budget. However, I cannot join a club until I have visited several, chosen one and requested support for membership application.

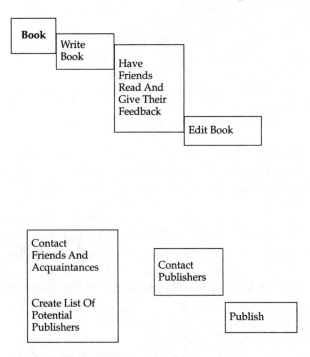

Figure 7.4 *Affinity map in time order: Book*

In the example of the book as shown in Figure 7.4, I can start exploring options around publishing at the same time as I start writing the book. However, I might choose not to contact publishers until I have finished editing it.

CREATING OBJECTIVES

You now have an ordered list of actions to take, each linked to the key elements in your vision. Before starting your full action plan you need to check back to your vision and conditions of satisfaction to ensure that you have clear objectives. Check that your objectives are SMART by asking the following questions:

- Specific – What is it you want to achieve?
- Measurable – What are the tangible results?
- Achievable – Are the results possible to achieve?
- Relevant – Do they relate to my vision?
- Timed – When will you have the results?

In the example I have been using these might be:

- Sports – Play tennis twice a week and earn a place in the top ten of the club's league table.
- Book – Sell 2,000 copies of my book by June 1999.

Now all you have to do is write the actions down in the left-hand column of the action plan on page 88 and colour in the blocks of time you think it will take and when you will do it. An example of an action plan is given on page 87. The shaded section indicates when action is to be taken.

The beauty of this type of chart is that you can maintain the dependencies and links between actions. For example, the chart clearly shows that I can create a budget and start saving at the same time. However, I cannot join the club until I have saved enough money. It acts as a double check on the links and affinities you found when doing your mind map and affinity map.

Also, it provides a quick monitoring tool in that you can draw a line down from the top to the bottom and see where you should be. For example, drawing a line down the middle of June shows the writing of the book should be finished, friends should have read it, and the editing should be almost complete.

SUMMARY

This chapter has really focused on getting into action. Getting the plans in place is half the job done. Often you do not start projects because they simply seem too big. This chapter has aimed to break those projects down into manageable steps that you can monitor.

ACTIONS	Feb	Mar	Apr	May	Jun	Jul	Aug	Sep	Oct
Book Sell 2000 Copies									
Write Book	▓	▓							
Friends Read			▓						
Edit				▓					
Contact Friends And Acquaintances		▓							
List Publishers		▓	▓						
Contact Publishers						▓	▓		
Publish								▓	▓
Sports 10 In League Twice A Week									
Visits Clubs	▓								
Choose Club		▓	▓	▓					
Application Support		▓							
Create Savings	▓	▓	▓	▓	▓	▓			
Create Budget	▓	▓	▓	▓	▓	▓			
Join Club							▓		
Commit To Friends							▓	▓	▓
Join Ladder						▓	▓	▓	
Book Lessons							▓	▓	
Buy New Racquet									▓

▓ This indicates when action is to be taken.

◄ **Know Yourself**

Now make your own action plan.

ACTIONS									

8 Confidence

Confidence is to be willing to try that which scares you most and the belief that you can manage anything that arises.

Would you like to have more self-confidence? Actually I have not yet met a person who replied to that question with a negative. We have all met people who seem to be very confident and probably wondered a little enviously how they got it. Well, there is only one way: by daring to do it. One of the ways you gain confidence is by trying things you are not sure you can do. Each time you achieve something new you boost your confidence levels a little.

Many times you are afraid to try new things because you could fail and that wouldn't look good. However, trying is what is most important. If you don't try, you have failed already so you have nothing to lose by trying. Not trying means you do not even give yourself the chance of succeeding. You stay in the safety zone of not looking silly or failing. It probably is safer but it also gets you nowhere. So the first step to building confidence is daring to try that which you are not sure you will succeed at. Don't forget to plan for your worst-case scenario before you do anything but remember that very rarely will that worst-case scenario ever become a reality.

Building self-confidence is also about what you should not be doing. For example, something happens and you end up looking silly and unprofessional. Most of you will spend some time worrying about it and thinking what you should have done instead. It is true you should learn from your mistakes, but there's no need to punish yourself for them. Remember, keep things in perspective and file it now. Having tolerance and compassion for yourself is just as important as having it for others.

SUBMISSION, CONFIDENCE AND ARROGANCE

There is a spectrum of behaviour ranging from submissive to arrogant, each with a different set of attitudes. Confidence sits in the middle of the spectrum. The focus and perspective of people change as they move along the spectrum. The confidence spectrum is shown in Figure 8.1.

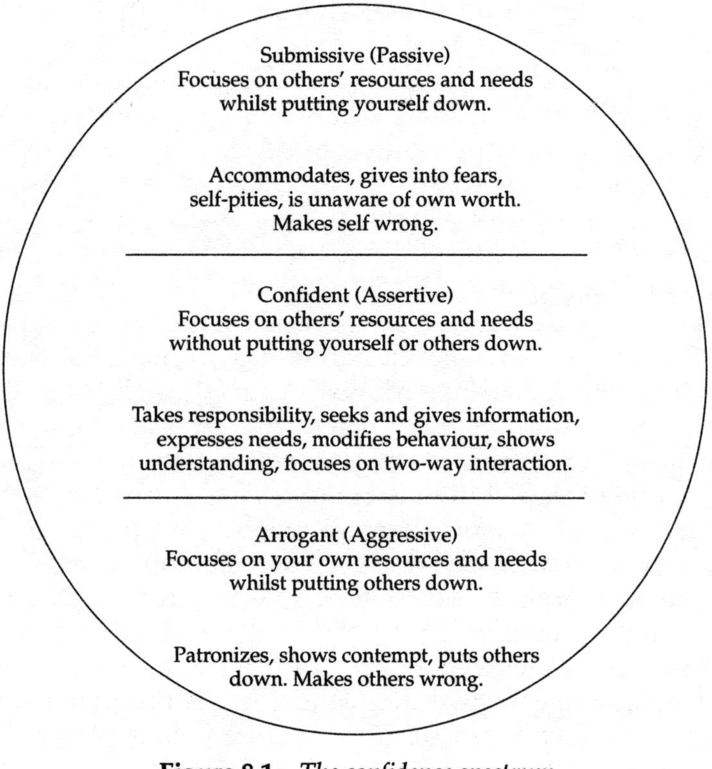

Submissive (Passive)
Focuses on others' resources and needs
whilst putting yourself down.

Accommodates, gives into fears,
self-pities, is unaware of own worth.
Makes self wrong.

Confident (Assertive)
Focuses on others' resources and needs
without putting yourself or others down.

Takes responsibility, seeks and gives information,
expresses needs, modifies behaviour, shows
understanding, focuses on two-way interaction.

Arrogant (Aggressive)
Focuses on your own resources and needs
whilst putting others down.

Patronizes, shows contempt, puts others
down. Makes others wrong.

Figure 8.1 *The confidence spectrum*

Think of people you know along the confidence spectrum, how do they behave? Place them somewhere along the line shown in Figure 8.2.

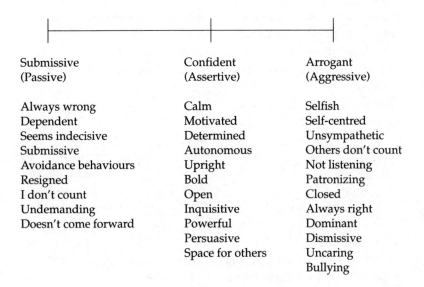

Submissive (Passive)	Confident (Assertive)	Arrogant (Aggressive)
Always wrong	Calm	Selfish
Dependent	Motivated	Self-centred
Seems indecisive	Determined	Unsympathetic
Submissive	Autonomous	Others don't count
Avoidance behaviours	Upright	Not listening
Resigned	Bold	Patronizing
I don't count	Open	Closed
Undemanding	Inquisitive	Always right
Doesn't come forward	Powerful	Dominant
	Persuasive	Dismissive
	Space for others	Uncaring
		Bullying

Figure 8.2   *Characteristics of the confidence spectrum*

Now decide where *you* want to be.

ENHANCING YOUR CONFIDENCE

Confidence is like a house that you need to build and maintain, regardless of who or what may be trying to damage it. To stretch the analogy, your house is vulnerable to the elements of nature. These elements will pound at the brickwork and, unless you protect it, the brickwork will eventually crumble. Your house will need to be able to withstand the elements.

The only way to gain self-confidence is through action. Like training to be an athlete, it requires a planned workout programme, the right mental state and stamina. To enhance your self-confidence there are two things to remember. First, it is about positively boosting your confidence. Second, it is about stopping the negativity that undermines your confidence. Gaining confidence is about changing your behaviour so that you create the image of confidence for yourself and others.

Often you assess your achievements and skills by how you think others will see them. This is self-defeating because how the world judges these things is often fickle. It changes its mind and doesn't necessarily always get it right (many artists are familiar with this painful truth).

So you rob yourself of confidence by undermining your successes. But you also undermine your confidence by crucifying yourself for your mistakes. Well, let's have a look at what you can do about it. First of all, you need to remember that you don't need to be perfect and that whatever you think people are thinking about you is probably a lot worse than what they really are thinking. When you make mistakes, you worry about what others will think, especially when their thoughts go against how you would like them to see you. It goes against the image you are trying to build. And that makes you feel like you have let yourself down. Here are some of the common confidence robbers and some of the things you can do to boost your confidence.

Your self-esteem must come from within, so don't use the world outside to judge something that must come from inside. The world will judge people differently according to the times and fashion. If you feel something is a skill or achievement, then it is, regardless of what others may think.

Protecting your confidence levels

There are several things you need to do to protect your confidence levels or, in other words, to prevent you from undermining your own confidence. For example, use your personal portfolio and remember to ask yourself, what do I think of the person described there? Look for the positive

Confidence robbers	Confidence boosters
Cognitive	
Selective perception	Focus on the good as well as the bad
Selective memory	Remember the good as well as the bad
Interpretation of events	Remember your interpretations may be
Believing bad events	wrong
will be repeated	Dare to defy the past
Unrealistic comparisons	Create a different future
Self-awareness	
Not aware of own worth	Keep generating your personal portfolio
Lack of belief in self	Know your worth
Reliance on the external	Be self-reliant for acknowledgement
Fear	
Failure	Plan for worst case scenario
Looking silly	Keep things in perspective
Being a disappointment	Failure is a learning experience
Fear of making mistakes	Use the handling mistakes process
Plan carefully	Identify your core belief
Letting yourself down	
Hiding 'the fraud'	Bankrupt the blackmailer
Lack of responsibility	Accept the consequences of your actions
Lack of commitment	Remember setbacks are temporary
Lack of possibility	Generate your vision

rather than the negative in situations and keep things in perspective.

Think of an event that dented your confidence, one where you really felt silly, failed, or simply should have done better. Go through the completion exercise and then think about how important this event will be in about six months. It probably won't feature that much, will it? So if you know that at one point you will file it into your memory bank, why not file it now? Better still, dump it. At least like that you won't suffer for the next six months. Why suffer at all, it doesn't change the event or the consequences? Don't keep looking back over it and analysing it. That won't change anything. You can't change the past but you can change the future.

Decide beforehand how long you are allowed to worry about something, worry for that time and then file it or dump it. Sometimes a friend can help you to keep to the time line.

If the event is really dire and you foresee serious consequences, plan for the worst-case scenario as you did in Chapter 5. When you know what you need to do, stop thinking about it and just do it. Sometimes you will get it wrong, and when you do, you need to handle the mistake. Figure 8.3 shows the steps to take to handle mistakes.

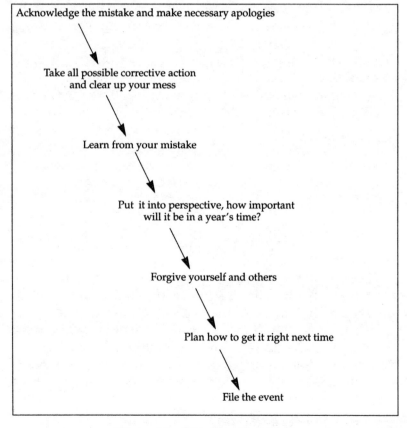

Figure 8.3 *Handling the mistake*

Building your confidence

Imagine that you are invited to a drinks party and you only know the person you arrived with. Do you wait for your companion to introduce you or do you go to people in the room and introduce yourself? Most people find the second of these options very difficult. It seems to be rude or imposing, especially when there is a small group who are obviously in conversation. Yet, this is one way to make a confident impression. Try it next time.

Most fears never materialize, for example, the fear of failure. Very rarely do you fail utterly at something and rarely does it have catastrophic consequences. All the catastrophe has already happened in your mind and that is why you don't face up to your fears.

Take a piece of paper and create a scale from 0 (not confident all) to 10 (very confident). Put yourself somewhere on that scale. You may want to consider different situations with different associated levels. For example, you may be confident with certain people and not others, or certain situations and not others. Figure 8.4 shows an example of the confidence scale.

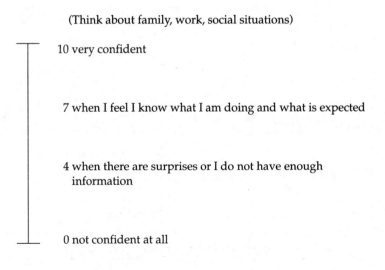

Figure 8.4 *Example of the confidence scale*

Now draw your own confidence scale.

(Think about family, work, social situations)

┬ 10 very confident

┴ 0 not confident at all

Now have a look at the difference between the situations or people that you feel more confident with as opposed to those where you do not. What are the differences?

You might like to pause here for a moment and consider how other readers of this book might have answered this question.

What makes you lose confidence?	
Fear of the unfamiliar	Fear of failing
Fear of looking silly	Fear of others' aggression
Fear of getting it wrong	Fear of standing up for your rights

There is only one way to get rid of fear and that is to face it.

> Running away or not facing your fears makes them all the stronger and you all the weaker.

Now for those occasions where things have gone wrong, remember the past does not necessarily dictate the future and there are certain steps you need to take. They say that when you fall off a horse the best thing to do is get right back on and try again. Actually, I think this is a good motto for life.

Perhaps you have a contribution to make in a meeting and are too shy, only to find someone else makes it and gets the credit. Think about how confident behaviour in that situation would be. What behaviour do you need to be displaying?

Once you know what it is about certain situations that shakes your confidence, try to take action to prevent being caught out by those situations. For example, do as much

The situation	How do I behave?
I don't speak up in meetings	Stay quiet
	Blush
	Get frustrated, then inarticulate when I do speak
	Just agree with others even when I have different opinions
	How would I like to behave?
	Give calm, informed, objective views
	Have well-qualified arguments
	Have my opinions heard

What do I need to do to behave the way I want to?
Be better prepared for meetings
Decide on my opinions beforehand
Build a case in my mind
Present solutions not problems
Keep talking till I am listened to
Ignore blushing, it doesn't change what I say

preparation as possible, ensure you have sought all possible information. And, for those times that you are still unprepared, make sure you have a coping strategy. For example, if you know being caught unprepared undermines your confidence, then generate a strategy that will give you time to compose yourself and take positive action. Compare the difference between how you behave now and how you would like to behave. This is called situational analysis, see above for an example of how it works.

The situation	How do I behave?
	How would I like to behave?

What do I need to do to behave the way I want to?

Remember, to achieve great things is like climbing a mountain. You can only do it by taking a step at a time. Breaking a task into small chunks makes it possible. Now fill in your own situational analysis.

SUMMARY

In this chapter you have explored how you undermine your confidence and what you can do to rebuild lost confidence. Now it is up to you to put into practice the principles which will maintain self-esteem and image. Below are the six key steps you will need to remember to build your confidence.

Step One

Know what you can contribute – use your personal portfolio.

Step Two

Keep the positive and negative in realistic balance – be objective.

Step Three

Declare your fear or area for improvement – face your fears.

Step Four

Check your interpretations for reality – only objective facts count.

Step Five

Handling mistakes – take responsibility, try again and file or dump it.

Step Six

Do what scares you most – plan for positive and worst-case scenarios.

TAKE ACTION – DO IT NOW

9 Case Studies

This has probably not been an easy book to read, so, I have created four fictional characters to help you on your way. I would like to introduce you to Sebastian, Clare, Roger and Susan. Each character is based on real-life situations taken from many different people who have followed this approach to achieving their vision. Their stories have been written to match the sequence of the chapters in the book, however, not all the exercises will appear in each case study.

SEBASTIAN

Sebastian is 36 years old, single and successful. He would very much like to have children and although he has a steady partner at the moment, he isn't sure if this is the right relationship. On the whole, he is very sociable but finds it hard to develop deep relationships with women.

The key events on Sebastian's life map were his parents divorce when he was 12, his arrival at boarding school two months after that and his career development, including the four promotions he received during the past few years. He was very quick to complete his life map.

After he had finished it he looked up proudly and went on to explain that he had achieved all of it despite the fact that his parents hadn't supported him. When asked about his experiences at school, he reluctantly admitted that he had hated it there and had found the transition from home to dormitory a very difficult one.

What was clearly missing from Sebastian's original life map was any reference to his personal life apart from the brief reference to his parents' divorce. Further exploration revealed that he had over the years several serious and intimate relationships. When talking about these relationships, Sebastian showed a significant degree of upset about losing some of them. He then quickly changed the subject to talk about his two best friends and some of the key events in his life with them. He had developed a close relationship with these two friends at school and over the years they had gained a deep trust and understanding of each other. After some discussion Sebastian went back and added quite a few events to his life map. Once it was fully completed it showed a much richer set of events and included the upsets around his personal relationships, his career success and his strong ties to his friends. Using his life map Sebastian had little difficulty with his personal portfolio.

Being courageous, Sebastian decided to ask his friends for the adjectives they would use to describe him for his perception tree. He was a little shocked to find out that although they perceived him as fun and loyal they also recognized a hard streak in him that could frighten or even alienate people. His sense of humour could at times be very sharp and cutting. This was not reflected in how he perceived himself at all. After some thought and analysis he admitted that at times he could be a little harsh especially with women that he was close to. In exploring the behavioural evidence he began to identify the exact behaviour patterns that gave him this image.

Sebastian has a very clear and understandable event cycle that has led to his behaviour patterns. He had found the whole deterioration of his parents' marriage very distressful, and often felt he was placed in the middle trying to mediate and negotiate between the two. He became a peace broker. He learnt how to see situations from different perspectives and how to present the common ground between these views. He had become the solution provider to his parents and always trod a careful path to ensure that neither his father nor his mother felt he was ever taking sides.

The hardest blow came when they sent him to boarding school. It was the one decision that both his parents had actually agreed on, leaving Sebastian feeling like neither of them wanted him, nor his help in solving their problems. Moreover, when he got to boarding school what he found was an environment where jostling for position was all important. During his time there he continued to develop relationships by being everyone's ally and thereby avoiding conflict. He trusted and relied only on the two people he considered his best friends. He had created a small space where he felt safe.

Watching his parents' relationship deteriorate he unconsciously decided that the same thing wasn't going to happen to him. He started to develop superficial relationships rather than deeper ones because he saw the deeper relationships as being potentially far more dangerous and hurtful.

As he grew older, he developed very sophisticated ways of ensuring that people liked him and cared for him without ever letting them get too close to him. This worked very well for him at school and early in his career. He became a good political player in the company, liked by most people. He also had excellent negotiating skills which furthered his career. This is one of the pay-offs of his behaviour.

As his friends were starting to get married and create families, he began to realize these were experiences he wanted to have too. The problem was that whenever he came close to having a deeper relationship with a woman, something would go wrong. He would usually find something about his partner or the relationship that made a long-term commitment impossible in his mind. At that point he would start to find fault with her and eventually drive her away. Rarely did he sit down to discuss the matter directly with her to try to resolve it.

This was the cost of Sebastian's behaviour patterns; he was pushing people away because that felt safer, but at the same time this prevented him developing any deep relationships that could lead to commitment and eventually a family. Direct discussion was also difficult because it might lead to conflict, so he chose to test his partners, pushing them away to see how long they would stay with him.

His inner thinking was that by testing his partner he could safeguard himself against the possibility of her leaving him. The problem was, of course, that from her point of view it just felt like he didn't want to be with her at all. On top of that his sharp sense of humour was often very painful and rather degrading.

It was clear that Sebastian had to make a choice on how to deal with the anger towards his parents for what he saw as their abandonment of him. Leaving matters as they were would make it very hard for Sebastian to understand, forgive and move on. His anger and fear would continue to get in the way of his future relationships. After serious deliberation and some hesitation, Sebastian decided he would talk to his parents about how he felt. The fear, of course, was that it would lead to confrontation.

Gathering all his strength, Sebastian had the conversations he needed to have and found out that the reason why his parents had agreed on sending him to boarding school was because they both shared one thing, their love for Sebastian. These conversations were hard because his parents naturally got a little defensive about what had happened, they initially felt accused of being bad parents. Everyone's emotions were causing friction and the temptation for Sebastian to give up was enormous. He kept trying and slowly his parents were able to explain that they had realized their relationship wasn't doing him any good and, in their minds, sending him to boarding school was the only way to get him out of being 'piggy in the middle'. Furthermore, they did not want him to have to go through a custody battle. They felt therefore that it was best for Sebastian to go to boarding school.

This gave Sebastian a different perspective and he began the slow and painful process of realizing that his parents are human beings, their intentions were good even though in Sebastian's reality it felt very different.

Sebastian was quite clear on his vision, he wanted to continue being successful at work, maintain his sense of humour but become more sensitive to the vulnerability of others and build a long-lasting relationship. For him there was only one major factor to focus on — give up testing his partners and be able to give them his trust. The words written here make it sound easy, but for Sebastian this was a major hurdle.

Now, at least, he could recognize his behaviour patterns and put together an action plan that gave him maximum chance of learning to communicate openly in his relationships. Don't underestimate the effort this took because for Sebastian it meant making himself vulnerable to his fear that his partner wouldn't really love him and would leave him. This meant facing the fear that had up till this point shaped his life.

Luckily, Sebastian had developed a talent in negotiation and mediation but had up till now only used it in the work place. He needed to be able to use these skills in his personal relationships. By going over recent negotiations he identified the specific skills and techniques he used there and found ways to transfer these to his personal relationships.

Also, having identified that when he felt threatened he would push people away, he put together a strategy that would allow him to explain this to his partner as well as giving her ways to recognize when he was doing it. In putting this into practice, he found admitting openly to his partner when he was feeling vulnerable created the space for an intimate conversation that allowed the relationship to develop further.

Given the enormous task that Sebastian undertook, he realized the likelihood of not maintaining his new behaviours was quite high. To avoid the damage this could cause he shared the situational analysis technique with his partner. This allowed them to focus together on his behaviour patterns and took out some of the emotion, as well as the need to prove who was right or wrong. It speeded up their conversations and, eventually, as they got more proficient in its use they used this as the basis for talking about their relationship and what each of them needed to do to make it a more fulfilling experience.

CLARE

Clare is 43 years old and has two children, a daughter called Christina and a son called John. Christina is 19 and John is 16. She has always been a housewife and mother and has no experience of working outside of that environment. Clare is experiencing a growing dissatisfaction with her life.

Clare's life map, in contrast to Sebastian's, focused totally on the relationships in her personal life, for example, when she met her husband, the birth of her children, the death of her father and her relationship changes with her mother. When asked to look back at her life map and think about events outside the family life she thought for a while and added the facts that she had become treasurer of the golf club two years ago and had a degree in Economics.

Sebastian's and Clare's life maps both show where they put the emphasis in their lives: both had left out crucial information which was pushed aside by what they saw as the key features of their lives. Sometimes what people leave out is as revealing as what they put into their life maps.

Clare easily recognized her maternal skills and qualities. She thought about her role in the family and listed all the skills and qualities she used there. It was quite an impressive list but not complete, as we shall see later. After having done her life map she was careful to include her degree and her work in the golf club as two of her achievements in her personal portfolio.

When Clare came to do her perception tree, her initial boxes were her friends, family and mother. I asked her about other relationships that she has with people who were not within this personal sphere. She thought long and hard and after a while created quite a list of other people she deals with in terms of the house, insurance, banks, and so on. In fact, Clare ran the house in its entirety including all the family's savings plans, and general finances. She had also managed from start to finish the refurbishment of the kitchen and bathrooms. We added these groups of people to her perception tree to provide both the personal and less personal relationships in her life.

What was interesting was that Clare felt she displayed quite different types of behaviour within each of these groups. For example, she tended to be quite firm and assertive with the board of the golf club. She was able to express herself clearly, influence them and deal efficiently with things when they went wrong.

In exploring the difference between how she believed others perceive her and how she perceived herself, we uncovered that she was in fact able to do much more than either she or her family seemed to recognize. Her family's, as well as her own, perception of her was limited to her household and maternal role. Clare revisited her personal portfolio and added the skills she had come to recognize as a result of looking a little more closely at her self-image and how she believed others perceived her.

Over a period of time, it became clear to Clare that she wanted to create an image that encompassed all the aspects she had discovered in completing her perception box and perception tree. She realized she wanted more recognition for her skills and attributes which she used outside of the home.

At this stage, Clare explained that her behaviour patterns inside the home and outside the home were different because she naturally perceived the environments to be very different. Rather like a chameleon she would adapt to her environment by changing her behaviour to what she saw as being appropriate at the time. Since she perceived the outside environment as more hostile, she was much more assertive there. After all, she didn't want them to take advantage of her.

Without realizing it Clare had established deep-rooted behaviour patterns that reflected what she thought people expected of her. She had adapted her behaviour in each situation to meet these expectations. The cost of this was that neither her needs nor her abilities were recognized. However, by constantly trying to meet people's expectations she received their acceptance and approval. Also by not declaring what she was capable of, she managed these expectations such that the risk of letting people down was minimal, a valuable pay-off.

We also spent a considerable amount of time looking at her relationship with her husband. She was very angry with him but was unclear as to why. Over the years she had always supported him but felt he rarely supported or acknowledged her. She had been getting more and more frustrated with him and as a result more and more angry.

During the discussion she suddenly went very quiet as she realized that actually she hadn't acknowledged him for what he was doing either. Also she hadn't told him what she had been feeling, not because she didn't want to, but because she hadn't quite put her finger on what she was feeling. How could her husband behave differently if she hadn't told him what she needed?

Clare took a stance to create more in her life. She wanted a job that would still allow her to focus on her family so it needed to have flexible hours. Office-based work wasn't what she wanted although she did want to work with people. She considered a flower shop, a charity and then in talking to one of her friends she came up with the idea of an estate agent. This would allow her to determine when she worked, not be tied to a desk all day and it meant she could work with people.

Clare's action plan was twofold, one to improve her relationship with her husband and two, to seek out what it would take to become an estate agent. One behaviour she decided to change was telling her husband about her day.

Usually when he came home she would listen to the events in his day and merely mention a few things about hers. Her husband never learnt about the negotiations with the workmen when they wanted to go to another job before completing what they were doing for Clare. Neither did he learn that Clare had saved the golf club a fair amount of money by suggesting some changes in how they managed their finances.

In talking about her relationship with her husband, Clare also brought up her relationship with her mother. The death of her father had been hard on both of them and their relationship had changed as a result. Clare had wanted to support her mother and allowed her mother to depend on her very heavily. This had two consequences, one that Clare didn't fully come to terms with her own loss and second, she felt responsible and guilty when her mother was upset and lonely. Instead of supporting her mother to rebuild her life, Clare had started trying to fill the space the death of her father had left for her mother. Over time she began unconsciously to resent this and the relationship became more and more strained. When she was feeling resentful, it just added to the guilt. As part of her action plan, Clare committed to talking to her mother about her own feelings about the loss of her father. Also she agreed to explore what her mother really needed from her in terms of support. In talking to her mother Clare had started the process of completing the past, leaving her free to get on with the future.

When Clare shared her action plan with her husband, he was initially a little surprised but after talking him through her vision he could begin to understand what she wanted and why. She also asked him for his support by making it very clear what she needed from him.

Clare had started the difficult process of overcoming the constraints she had placed on herself. She accepted the challenge of creating her life to include the expectations she had of herself. Her greatest obstacle was the struggle to give up her need to meet others' expectations. She had to keep reminding herself of what she was trying to achieve and not feel guilty about wanting to achieve it. Having stepped out of her safety zone and declared what she was capable of, she now had to face the fear of delivering her promise.

ROGER

Roger is 48 and a father of four. He has worked in the same company for the last fifteen years and feels frustrated with his career. He is very family-orientated and wishes he could spend more time at home. He has recently been feeling quite tired but feels it will pass with time. He directly manages a team of five and is well respected within the business as a man who gets things done. Roger feels like he is failing in his marriage as at work.

Seeing Roger's personal portfolio it was apparent that he had difficulty with the achievements list and only came up with his engineering degree, his family and the house he had bought as the three achievements he recognized.

In discussion Roger was very quick to point out all the things he had not achieved, like the promotion he had gone for but did not get. Also he named several projects that had failed to deliver all they should have done.

After considerable questioning and encouragement it turned out that over the years he had achieved a high service level award for a specific project he had managed. This project had saved the company £750,000 over a four-year period and last year he had received a large bonus in recognition of his commitment to the company.

In Roger's case, what he is clearly doing is negating his achievements and focusing on the failures of his life. Once he had fully completed his personal portfolio and sat back to realize he'd created a description of himself, he fell silent and then smiled.

He was always driving himself very hard and would put in long hours at work and then cram his weekends with activities with, and for, the family. He usually had very little time for himself or indeed time to just relax, sit back and rest. As a result he often felt tired and would become a little short-tempered at home when things went wrong. At work he had also been known to bark at people when he felt they weren't performing to the best of their ability. Whenever he did this he would regret it and feel guilty at what he had just done. He knew there were perhaps better ways of tackling the situation but would find it hard in the moment to muster the strength to behave differently.

Roger treats life very seriously and himself in it. He doesn't easily tolerate mistakes and certainly works very hard to avoid failure. He often disregards his success and tends to focus on the negative rather than the positive. He sees his role in life as being a strong provider for the family and wants to be seen as successful in his career.

He recounted the story of the promotion that he lost. He had been working very hard on several projects and wanted to prove that he was capable of more. He knew he was tired and a little stressed but where he worked that was not the kind of thing you admitted. At the time he was so absorbed in his work that often he would go in at weekends leaving him feeling like he was letting his family down. He was beginning to feel like he was neither the father and husband he wanted to be, nor were the projects at work really going as smoothly as he would have liked.

Finally, when word came through that he had not received the promotion he had been working so hard to get, his initial disappointment quickly changed to anger. He had put in all this energy, had jeopardized his family life, and for what? He forgot all the positive aspects of his career before that time and concentrated only on the last failure.

Upon deeper reflection it transpired that Roger's anger was rooted in disappointment with himself for not being able to manage all the aspects of his life in the way that he wanted. He recognized that in the months prior to the promotion he had been displaying symptoms of stress. He had not been sleeping well, was easily irritated and some-times lost concentration.

It was hard for Roger to admit this as for him it equated to failure and in his beliefs of the world that was not permissible. In his hidden self he believed he was a failure and therefore worked very hard to be a success. His interpretations always focused on his failures thereby strengthening his inherent belief that he was a failure. His outward behaviours were all geared to being successful, that was how he got the reputation for being a man who gets things done. His need to avoid failure determined all his actions. The fear was controlling him rather than him controlling the fear. To take back his personal power he first needed to recognize all that he had achieved and where he had been successful. This was a major difficulty for Roger and he needed to remind himself every day to keep the positive and negative in balance. He also needed to re-establish what was important to him and what his own criteria of success were. What he came to realize was that if he had got the promotion it would have meant longer hours and less time for his family.

The core of the problem was that although he did not wish to be seen as not being able to handle the work, the truth was that he was being torn between wanting to be the perfect family man and the perfect professional. With only twenty-four hours in the day he needed to decide where his priorities lay and how to best manage those. He knew that he had been displaying signs of stress and had worked all the harder to make sure no one would suspect that he was over-working himself. This only served to create a downward spiral whereby the stress and loss of concentration led to mistakes which he then had to work even harder at to correct.

The fact of the situation was that he hadn't got the promotion. Although there was no denying this, his interpretation that this was because his boss didn't value him, or saw him as not being capable of the job, didn't necessarily hold true. Roger struggled a long time before he could see that there might be other interpretations. For example, there were other facts that Roger initially forgot to mention, like the person they brought in was from a different organization all together.

One possible interpretation could be that Roger was indeed seen as incapable of taking on the promotion. Alternatively, it could be that the company simply couldn't afford to lose Roger from his present job because that would leave them vulnerable in that area of business. Roger found it hard to discuss this with his boss because he was so convinced that his interpretation was right.

As it happened, Roger's boss called him into the office about a week later to discuss the organizational structure. He explained that they had thought long and hard about the promotion and in the end decided that they needed a quick transition and that Roger was so involved in his projects that there wasn't time to effect a hand-over to one of his subordinates. What transpired in the conversation that followed was that over the years Roger's need to make sure everything was correctly done and successfully completed had led him to adopting a very hands-on style of management. This meant that he was often involved in work that really his team should and could have taken care of. Roger needed to learn more about how to delegate and how to develop his staff so they were in the position to take over from Roger when the next opportunity arose.

The pay-off for Roger of keeping a hands-on style of management was that he could ensure success. The cost was that he was losing time doing things that he didn't need to be doing, thus leaving less time for other things that perhaps were more important.

What we can learn from Roger's case is that things happen in life over which we do not always feel we have full control. What is important is how we deal with them. We can get angry and we can blame ourselves or others for these events. As with Roger, initially these are natural reactions and have their place, but they shouldn't remain the basis for a coping strategy.

At some point you will have to deal with the situation and take responsibility for it. The moment you do, you are back in control. Roger decided that it was time for him to accept what had happened and that he needed to forgive himself and others and move on. It was time for him to take a positive look at where he wanted to go from here.

The need to avoid failure had been a driving force in Roger's life for a long time. It was time for him to decide whether he was going to let this need drive him or whether he was going to drive his needs. The only way to do this was to accept his past successes. Also he needed to be able to accept his failures for what they were by putting them into perspective. Looking back over his life, his successes far outweighed his failures.

Roger had maintained a strict hands-on approach to management because when his people failed he failed, yet he needed to learn to be able to take that risk and to let go. In letting go of the fear he was able to delegate and thereby develop his team. He also freed up some time which he spent thinking more strategically about his area of business. Finally, he questioned his need for the promotion and although he didn't want to give that up as part of his vision, it took a position more equal to other things in his life. Letting go of the fear did not mean Roger lost his fear, it was always there but he consciously had to face it and learn to take appropriate risks.

SUSAN

Susan is 19 and works as a secretary. She is attending a course in business studies during the evenings. She is hardworking, creative and enthusiastic but finds it hard to communicate and get her ideas across in the office. She feels she is ignored and often her ideas aren't taken seriously. Susan often worries about what other people think of her.

Susan has an older brother and sister and one sister who is younger than herself. Her life map showed her childhood and home life as happy and comfortable. Home was always busy and hectic with everyone speaking at the same time but rarely being heard. Family events were always disorganized but fun. Her older brother and sister had often been left in charge of the younger children which continued even as the younger ones became older.

Susan's problem with her personal portfolio arose from the fact that she felt she was young and as such had little to offer, although she was quite clear about her qualities. When asked for evidence of these qualities, she could recount various stories and events of where she had struggled and triumphed to get what she wanted. However, she qualified all her achievements with an explanation of why they had been difficult to achieve. Susan found it extremely hard to simply mention them with pride without feeling she had to justify why each was an achievement. She was unable to rely on her own judgement and decision of what was an achievement for her and felt only the things she had really struggled for counted. When she realized this, she was able to come up with a bigger list of achievements and she was then in a position to start looking at the skills she had used to make these happen.

Susan experienced little trouble in describing how she perceived herself or how she thought others perceived her and the two were quite consistent, but what did re-occur in both sets of perceptions was that she saw herself and believed others saw her as timid.

All four of our characters spent quite some time looking at what they had learnt from doing their perception trees. Specifically, they looked at the behavioural evidence to see how they might be creating some of the perceptions they recognized.

Susan in particular discovered that she had good ideas but would not voice them clearly in meetings. She would offer her opinion but would often be interrupted or ignored. She rarely stood up for herself on these occasions and just sat quietly only to hear her thoughts expressed by someone else. What she found hardest was that often others got the credit for an idea that she had tried to interject. Somehow when others shared ideas the group listened.

Susan's perception of herself was that she was not

assertive and unable to express her ideas or influence people. She remembered an incident where she went with her older sister to a party. She wanted a drink but the hostess asked her older sister first who declined the offer and Susan was never asked. She was too shy to say anything at the time and therefore was left without a drink.

This was not the only time she remembered feeling left out, ignored or not listened to. What she decided about the world and herself in it was that her needs and her concerns were not worth being heard. She learnt not to push her thoughts forward because she got hurt every time they were ignored. With hindsight and further analysis Susan realized that as a child she had been naturally timid and her sister had often spoken up for her to protect and take care of her. Her older sister felt responsible for Susan and therefore naturally took over in situations when Susan seemed uncomfortable or shy.

In the early years this felt quite normal and comfortable for Susan because it allowed her to avoid dealing with people directly. This was the pay-off. Of course, as Susan grew older she wasn't getting what she wanted, she was getting what her sister wanted or what her sister thought she wanted. This became a cost.

The full cost of her behaviour pattern became even more evident when she started work in that she was still seen as timid and others were getting the credit for her ideas. To begin to change her image Susan first took responsibility for allowing her sister to speak for her. She had to accept that she had created survival mechanisms which used her sister as a buffer between herself and the world. Susan found this uncomfortable as it meant admitting something about herself that she didn't like.

Next was the battle to realize it wasn't that her ideas weren't worth hearing as she believed, it was that she hadn't ever really stood up for her thoughts, ideas, opinions or beliefs. She started to practise some basic assertiveness techniques. For example, in meetings she learnt to time her comments more appropriately. She analysed meetings and found that they had stages. For example, there is little point in stating a solution to a problem while everybody else is still in the fact-finding stage. More difficult for Susan was to learn to present her ideas clearly. She started by practising at home prior to meetings. She would also think about who was going to be in the meeting and how they might feel about the ideas she was presenting. She explained to a colleague what she was trying to achieve and asked for feedback directly after meetings to see where she might improve her influencing skills.

During this process Susan discovered another behaviour pattern that she had developed over the years. She would often analyse and worry endlessly about conversations she had had with people. She would try to guess what they might be thinking about her. This was particularly acute when she felt she had made a mistake or done something silly. She was being held ransom by her blackmailer. In her hidden self she felt not only the ideas weren't worth hearing but that perhaps they were stupid in the first place. Susan took several actions to create a strategy that would have her stop worrying so much. She revisited the handling mistakes exercise and also agreed to set aside a certain amount of time that she was allowed to worry. After this time had elapsed she had to decide to either go and find out how others had seen the situation or she had to dump it.

One thought that helped Susan was that most people are more concerned about their own image than they are about others. Think about the people around you, they probably spend only a small amount of time thinking about you and your mistakes because they are far too busy thinking about their own.

The actions Susan embarked on were not easy and, as you can no doubt appreciate, this was not an overnight process. Susan had to work very hard to keep fighting her own self-image and spend time being the person she wanted to become.

10 What's Next?

By now you will have a very good idea of who you are; where you want to go and what you need to do to get there. As a quick summary, below are the key tools, techniques and concepts you have used. Each is described by its purpose or outcome.

Tool/techniques/concept	Purpose/outcome
Life map	Understanding the key influences in your life
Personal portfolio	Exploring what you have to contribute
Balancing positive and negative	Maintaining confidence, acknowledging what is good
Self-perception box	Exploring your self-image
Perception tree	Exploring others' image of you
Behavioural analysis	Collecting behavioural evidence to support your image
The blackmailer	Exploring that which you are afraid to show
The event cycle	Understanding your view of the world

Collecting evidence	Exploring the objective basis for your world view
From evidence to meaning	Understanding why stories are not always objective
Perspective taking	Staying objective
Completing the past	Letting go of baggage
Pay-offs and costs of behaviours	Your logical basis for choice of action
Worst-case scenarios	Facing your fears reduces their power over you
Vision drawing	Know where you want to go
Mind maps	Linking key elements
Affinity map	Pulling all your thoughts together
The action plan	Knowing how you are going to achieve your vision
Handling mistakes	Clearing the mess and moving on

Having spent a fair amount of energy exploring yourself and your life you are hopefully now committed to taking action. You have started your journey but probably have not yet reached your destination.

Given that none of us live in isolation, we need to consider how your environment may react to you as you try to change your behaviour patterns, manage your image and achieve your vision.

Let's say that one of the things you have chosen to do is to take more responsibility. In terms of the behaviour patterns that you might be looking to change, you are aiming to stop complaining, talking to third parties about someone else in the hope that they might do something about it and you are pro-actively seeking to find solutions to problems that you see around you.

As you start to change, you will experience various reactions from others around you. Remember, others may not have read this book or gone through the process that you have just been through. They may be where you were when you started this book and therefore will not understand everything that you are up to. You are likely to experience three different types of reactions from those around you. One, you change and nobody seems to notice, they just keep on treating you as they always did. Two, you change your behaviour and they change theirs to match it. Three, you change and feel that others are trying to undermine your efforts.

The first type of reaction, or rather non-reaction, you might get is that no one seems to notice. This can feel worse than someone trying to undermine your efforts, at least they noticed something was different. When people don't notice, you can tell them what you are trying to achieve and ask them for feedback as to how you are doing. Be gentle with them because the request for feedback will hit them like a thunderbolt given they hadn't noticed any change in the first place. Also depending on their self-image, they may feel guilty that they hadn't noticed for themselves.

The second type of reaction you might get is that other people match your efforts. This, of course, is the best you could hope for. Not only have they noticed but they have put time and effort into redefining their relationship with you and how they need to interact with you. They might not get it a 100 per cent right but it's a great foundation for mutual support.

Last but by no means least, the third reaction you might get is that others seem to be undermining your efforts. Some people will feel threatened by how they see you changing and the increased level of control and power you are able to show. They might seek to undermine what you are achieving by pointing out where your efforts are failing. You need to remember that these people are not trying to undermine you personally. They are simply scared of the changes that they see in you and are no longer sure of how to interact with you. You have changed the rules of the game. They know the relationship they had with you is no longer there, but they are unsure of what the new relationship looks like and even more unsure as to how they should behave in that relationship. As you change your behaviour and your perspectives of the world, you may find that some of the people aren't who you thought they were.

You need to decide whether you are committed to the relationship. If you are, you need to support these people to redefine their relationship with you. However, you sometimes may need to let go, as there is often a divide between people who take responsibility for their lives and people who do not. That is because they each approach life from quite opposite directions and often one will get upset by or frustrated with the other. You may find that when you take full responsibility for your life, you lose patience with some of the people you know. You can now see that what they are doing is avoiding taking responsibility. Responsibility is truly scary for some people. This is fine if they let you get on with it. However, if they are trying to prevent you from getting on with your life, then it may well be time for you to review the relationship and set it within different parameters.

If you have a partner, it is always a good idea to involve them in the changes you are making to your life. They share your life and the changes you make are likely to affect them as much as you. They need to be reassured that you are not trying to change them or 'improve' them. You might be trying to improve the relationship that you have with them but never make them feel like they aren't good enough. In sharing with your partner it would help for you to clearly communicate your vision, what you are trying to achieve and why. Let them know how your behaviour is likely to change and explore with them how that might affect the relationship.

It is crucial that you don't fall into the common trap of expecting or wanting them also to change. Many times in self-development, after we have struggled and suffered through the process, we want those we care about to do the same. We can see the benefits that they would get out of it and become determined to show them the light. This is a fatal mistake in that people can only take on the process of self-exploration when they are ready to do so. By all means share with them what you got out of it and paint them a picture of what it is they might get out of it, but then leave them to think it through and make their own decisions. Should they decide that it is not for them, respect that decision. People will only change when the cost of that change is lower than the cost of maintaining their present behaviour. Or to put it another way, the pay-off of the change is higher than the pay-off of their present behaviour. Fear acts as a great deterrent to change and is often the most salient cost of change.

Your partner, family and friends make up a group of people who can often make a big difference to achieving or blocking your vision. As you start to move towards your vision they will naturally want to support you. However, there may be a part of them that also has a vision which they know they aren't making any steps towards getting. This may leave them with a dilemma in that they want you to succeed but at the same time feel left out and left behind. They may well exhibit behaviour that on the surface feels negative. Often what these people are really expressing is their inner desire to also strive for their vision.

In addition to how others might react to you, there are other issues that you will need to consider as you move towards your destination. Identify for yourself the most likely causes or events that could be the reason for you to give up on your vision. Make sure you consider these issues carefully so that you are able to recognize the symptoms of you beginning to get tired, questioning your vision or giving up. Don't get me wrong, you can change and alter your vision at any time but be sure you do so for the right reasons.

Now think about how you will deal with these situations when they arise. For all of you striving for a vision there are times when you won't be able to see the end of the tunnel and everything seems to be going against you. If you are not ready to deal with these times, they are likely to get the better of you rather than the other way round.

The easiest way to see this is like a board game where you need to do or collect certain things before you can move forward on the board. Perhaps it is a little like snakes and ladders, in that it can sometimes feel like you are making great strides forward and, then, on other occasions it feels like you are slipping back, sometimes further back than where you started. On these occasions, pick yourself up and take another turn. The point is not to walk away from the game, because as long as you are playing you will be moving and eventually you will reach the end of the game successfully. The point of the game I am describing here is not to be the first to get to the end. The point is to reach the end. Then you can start all over again as self-development, of course, never ends.

When it feels like you have slipped back a few squares you must first try to identify where you have slipped back to. Start with your vision, is it still what you want, if not, create what you do want and start the action planning process again.

As I said, the point is not to stop playing the game. There is a quick flow chart you can use to make sure that when you fall out of the process you can get yourself back into it. When things look bleak, ask yourself the following questions in the flow chart and take the appropriate action. You will then be back in the game.

Remember, when it starts to get tough, come back to the book, review the exercises, check your commitment and KEEP GOING UNTIL YOU GET WHERE YOU WANT TO BE.

A final point to changing things in your life is to ask yourself three questions. A negative response to any one of these three will be enough to throw your best-laid plans to the wind.

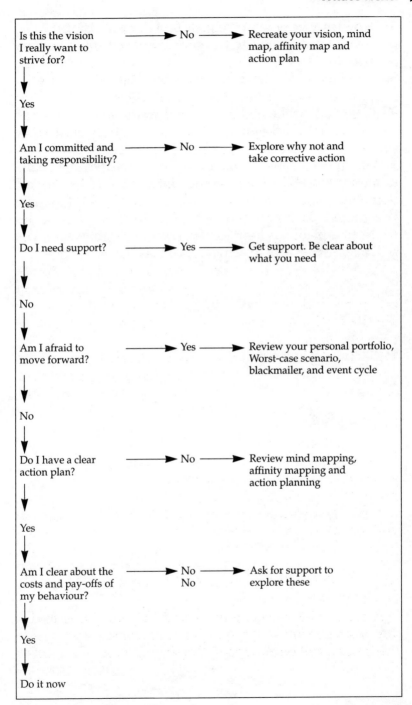

Is this the vision I really want to strive for? ———▶ No ———▶ Recreate your vision, mind map, affinity map and action plan

↓

Yes

↓

Am I committed and taking responsibility? ———▶ No ———▶ Explore why not and take corrective action

↓

Yes

↓

Do I need support? ———▶ Yes ———▶ Get support. Be clear about what you need

↓

No

↓

Am I afraid to move forward? ———▶ Yes ———▶ Review your personal portfolio, Worst-case scenario, blackmailer, and event cycle

↓

No

↓

Do I have a clear action plan? ———▶ No ———▶ Review mind mapping, affinity mapping and action planning

↓

Yes

↓

Am I clear about the costs and pay-offs of my behaviour? ———▶ No ———▶ Ask for support to explore these
No

↓

Yes

↓

Do it now

1. Do I truly believe in the possibility of my vision?
2. Have I communicated everything to all the necessary people?
3. Am I ready for the obstacles to my success?

Well, you are at the end of the book and you now have all the tools and techniques you will need to create and achieve your vision.

Remember, change is a hard thing to achieve and maintain and you will no doubt encounter the odd brick wall. Sometimes it will all feel like too much of a struggle and you might start to question why you are doing any of this in the first place. As long as you keep trying, however, you will be on your way to achieve your vision.

Index